Marital Love and Hate

Marital
Love and Hate

THE NEED FOR A REVISED
MARRIAGE CONTRACT AND
A MORE HONEST OFFER BY
THE MARRIAGE COUNSELOR
TO TEACH COUPLES TO
LOVE *AND* HATE,
HONOR *AND* DISHONOR,
OBEY *AND* DISOBEY

Israel W. Charny, Ph.D.

The Macmillan Company, New York, New York
Collier-Macmillan Ltd., London

The Macmillan Company
866 Third Avenue, New York, N.Y. 10022
Collier-Macmillan Canada Ltd., Toronto, Ontario

Library of Congress Catalog Card Number: 74–175592

First Printing

Printed in the United States of America

acknowledgments

We appreciate the following permissions to quote passages from other books or publications and other human sources:

From *The Politics of Experience* by R. D. Laing, Penguin Books, London, 1967.

From the magazine, *Fellowship*, published by the Fellowship of Reconciliation, Nyack, New York, a quotation by Maurice Friedman.

From *The Annals of the American Academy of Political and Social Science*, Philadelphia, a quotation from a paper by Elton B. McNeil.

From *Jewish Marriage Anthology* by Philip and Hanna Goodman, Jewish Publication Society, Philadelphia, 1965.

From *Lady Chatterley's Lover* by D. H. Lawrence. Text from the third manuscript version, first published by Giuseppe Orioli, Florence, 1928. Reprinted courtesy of Grove Press, New York; also, Laurence Pollinger Limited, London, Authors' Agents and the Estate of the late Mrs. Frieda Lawrence, and William Heinemann Ltd., London.

From *Mindswap* by Robert Sheckley. Copyright 1966 by Robert Sheckley. Reprinted by permission of the publishers, Delacorte Press, New York, and Victor Gollancz, London.

From the *National Enquirer*, Englewood Cliffs, New Jersey, an article by Joseph Cassidy from the November 16, 1969 issue.

From *Parade, The Sunday Newspaper Magazine*, an item from "Intelligence Report" edited by Lloyd Shearer, June 29, 1969.

A delightful, unsolicited letter to me from my colleague, Barry Bricklin, Ph.D.

The permission of some quite unidentified patients who saw sections describing them in advance and were good enough to agree to my use of these descriptions of our experience together.

Many of the ideas presented here were first developed at a family workshop organized by the Family Service of Chester County, West Chester, Pennsylvania, on September 27, 1967, under the title "Love and hate, honor and dishonor, obey and disobey in cooperative non-violent tension!: The need for a revised marriage contract and a revised offer of help by the marriage counselor."

A paper based on the above material appeared in the professional journal, *Family Process*, under the title "Marital love and hate" (Volume 8, Number 1, March, 1969, pages 1–24).

The larger concept of injustice in all of family life, including the marital relationship, was developed in two papers:

"Injustice and betrayal as natural experiences in family life" was presented to a conference on Family Therapy and Family Life Cycle sponsored by the Family Institute of Philadelphia, Pennsylvania, in May, 1969, and will be appearing in the journal, *Psychotherapy: Theory, Research, and Practice*.

"Terrors of annihilation in family life—and as training ground for terrors of annihilation in the larger world" was presented to a conference on The Child in his Family organized by the International Association for Child Psychiatry and Allied Professions, Jerusalem, Israel, August, 1970.

Several other professional publications by the author in the area of family therapy and in the larger area of man's genocidal destructiveness may be found among the references provided in the appendix.

To . . . . all of us

about the style of this book

One of the saddest, most wasteful, and ultimately destructive qualities of so many families' lives is their very flattening of life through the avoiding of feelings.

Books can also be accomplices to an over-intellectual flattening of life's *real* vibrancy.

Or, more correctly, readers can use books to aid and abet their avoidance of life.

But books can also help readers toward their potential for feeling and experiencing themselves.

Our own wishes for this work are twofold.

We hope our book represents a worthwhile contribution to the think world we love and believe it to be potentially valuable to man, namely, to theory building in psychology.

And we also are hoping this work encourages many readers to genuine experiences of their feelings, and to a new confidence in their being able to employ or channel these feelings wisely in their own best interests.

As something of a reflection of these two—we think, deeply interrelated—sides of the author's intentions, there follow as it were two books, the first, a book of theory, and the second, a book of practicalities.

Yet, we are hoping the book of theory also *reads-feels* like a stimulus for emotional experiencing (and we have been encouraged that this might be the case by a surprising number of reports from colleagues offered in response to the original journal paper, "Marital love and hate"—that various patients and clients found it good feeling-reading—even though the paper was written in reasonably standard science-journal style and included in large part a sober, workmanlike effort at seeing where the psychological literature of marriage was at these days).

And we hope that even the more serious, ascetic-like scientific-type reader will also find in book two's more swinging-loose "manual" of ideas for everyday marital loving and hating a good many conceptualizations that are on the level of the theoretical writing of the first book.

Perhaps the unity of feeling and thinking toward which we are striving will also support the very unity of loving and hating with which this book concerns itself.

about this unity of loving and hating

It seems appropriate in this introductory note to make it clear that the intent of our work is to help us all to *love* better —in the simplest, old-fashioned sense of the word.

It is not at all that we are agin' the old-fashioned values: to treasure the other, and cherish and care and adore and desire and admire and understand . . . and all those loving qualities we would all be.

The trouble is it isn't that simple.

And although we are far, far from understanding what it is all about, this symphony of humanness of which loving and the wish to love are beautiful but incomplete parts, we have come to believe there is a lot more hope for good, enduring *loving* when it comes out of an intense intermix with its more darkly, evil-colored antagonist *hating*.

For many good people, or at least well-intending people, *hating* is a terrible word.

In many families and cultures, a *no-no*.

As if the words of hate are equal to their deeds (which is not true).

As if hating meant not loving the object of one's hate (which is not true).

Let it be irrevocably clear that the goal of this book is to explore how we might better enjoy and support one another in our marriages:

to LOVE (hate)

—in ways that our hating supports, energizes, and backs up our loving to emerge as a more enduring, effective giving to one another; and

to HATE (love)

—so that our loving serves to temper our so-ready hating

of the other with a continuous awareness of the beauty and goodness and innocence of that very accursed other.

Because the hating side is the newer and more paradoxical and less understood, much of this book will treat of hating; and thus it might be construed that we are weighing more heavily the negative side of love-hate.

We do in fact have the strong impression that in the great inner tracking-stations of man, at any given time negative emotions take precedence over their positive counterparts of equal strength; the emotional agenda of us human beings will often *look like* there is more hating to be done than the loving we see as waiting, oh, so hopefully, to follow.

The important point here is, to be entirely clear, we mean throughout *loving and hating* whenever we refer to either.

Despite our far greater attention to the negative, the sometimes-shock meanings we develop, and our still deep uncertainties how to put together these forces which our culture and language teach us to pose violently against each other, we mean throughout to assist all of us to be closer in genuine and rewarding intimacy.

about other types of marrying
other than marrying

This is an age of profound question and challenge of the very institution of marriage. Personally, we are very much committed to the search for how to strengthen us all in the traditional marital experience, but we should add that we have no wish to exclude those who would experiment with entirely new institutional and societal forms.

There are many such experiments that are not our cup of brandy. Many we mistrust deeply. And some whose time has passed for us, though we imagine we would have enjoyed their brandy had it been available at an earlier time in our life. But, overall, we do understand and respect the need for such experiments; the lack of discussion of such alternatives in this book simply means we are busy enough trying to figure out how to tap the potential for intimacy and effective cooperation in more traditional marriage.

Which—we might also add—we have a hunch will remain the natural style for people even amidst a great many alternative styles of relating and intimacy, especially for young people prior to their undertaking a more serious effort at family life built around a traditional one-to-one marriage.

appreciations

I am deeply grateful to my secretary and professional assistant of some years, Mrs. Lillian Diffenderfer, for her steadfast help in preparing most of the original talks and journal articles from which this book has grown; I am particularly grateful to Lil for the many disarmingly commonsense ways in which she has supported and freed me to search for my further creativity.

The actual work of putting together this manuscript was that of Mrs. Frances Johnston for whose excellence of skill, as well as her pleasant sincerity, I am very appreciative.

It should be clearly understood that these statements of appreciation are in express violation of the wishes of both ladies not to be publicly identified with this dirty book.

an old-fashioned table of contents

About the Author

Marital Love and Hate

Book One

a book of "psychophilosophy"—
or a theoretical model

MARITAL HAPPINESS: WHEN HUSBAND AND WIFE CAN FIGHT EACH OTHER—WISELY

Ask most people how they picture a good marriage, and they are likely to wish up an image of a husband and wife cooperating warmly and thoughtfully; and if occasionally they must fight, they do so briefly, with little emotional excess, and never in front of the children. Ask most people how marriage counselors and psychotherapists seek to help people whose marriages are troubled, and they are likely to imagine a therapist trying to teach people how to be warm, thoughtful, and mature—and rid themselves of whatever emotional handicaps stop them from cooperating with their spouses.

Ask most professional mental-health counselors the same questions, and their answers will be wordier, but pretty much the same—hinting piously that a state of reasonableness and quiet awaits those couples who are wise enough to shed their infantile emotions.

Not so!

Only rarely does one hear the more honest acknowledgment that not only do virtually all marriages go through a great deal of hell for a good number of years (and should!), *but also the very, very few that really "make it" involve more openness for husband and wife to be angry at each other, honestly, with a fair amount of feeling—though with good control— and, yes, indeed, very much in front of the kids too* (although, admittedly, not quite as freely as some of the whoopdinger fights away from the kids).

Otherwise, these kids too would later join the millions of people who don't have the slightest idea how a husband and wife might fight with each other —effectively!

. . . when violence masquerades, as love, once the fissure into self and ego, inner and outer, good and bad occurs, all else is an infernal dance of false dualities. It has always been recognized that if you split Being down the middle, if you insist on grabbing *this* without *that*, if you cling to the good without the bad, denying the one for the other, what happens is that the dissociated evil impulse, now evil in a double sense, returns to permeate and possess the good and turn it into itself.

When the great Tao is lost, spring forth benevolence and righteousness.

When wisdom and sagacity arise, there are great hypocrites.

When family relations are no longer harmonious, we have filial children and devoted parents.

When a nation is in confusion and disorder, patriots are recognized.

—R. D. LAING. *The Politics of Experience.* New York: Pantheon Books, 1967, pp. 48–49.

Why are people cruel and why are they nice? Evil people are rare, but you find evil behavior in the majority of people.

—ABRAHAM H. MASLOW. *Psychology Today,* July, 1968, p. 35.

Until we learn to admit and live constantly with the fact that we commit violence against ourselves and others everyday, . . . we will make little progress.

—THOMAS S. KNIGHT. Violence and the phenomenon. *American Journal Orthopsychiatry,* 1969, *39,* p. 230.

The Hasidic rabbi Abraham applies this teaching to the wars of Frederick King of Prussia who fell on his enemy from the rear rather than directly attacking him: "What is needed is not to strike straight at Evil but to withdraw to the sources of divine power, and from there to circle around Evil, bend it, and transform it into its opposite." This means that evil itself can be redeemed and transformed into the good. True reconciliation from this standpoint does not mean ignoring evil or escaping from it, but confronting it and redeeming it. . . .

One must serve God with the "evil urge" as well as the good, says the Talmud.

—MAURICE FRIEDMAN. Hasidism and the love of enemies, a new approach to reconciliation. *Fellowship,* November, 1964.

... the comprehension of individual or group violence will continue to be a mystery if the form of development of human personality and the form to which human psychic structure can be modeled are treated as nothing more than an annoying gadfly pestering the concept of large-scale violence. The complexity of the human psyche has made it so forbidding an area of exploration that modern theorists have discounted human personality as an important influence in the affairs of mankind. . . . Yet, denying that the psychological nature of man has relevance in understanding human violence has produced only a bankrupt and barren vision of the future of humanity. Man's psychic nature cannot remain an unknown in the equation of violence or we will find ourselves presiding over the dissolution of the human race.

—ELTON B. McNEIL. Violence and human development. In Marvin E. Wolfgang (Ed.), *Patterns of Violence. The Annals of the American Academy of Political and Social Science*, 1966, p. 157.

Love and Hate . . . may perhaps have some fundamental relation to the polarity of attraction and repulsion (in physics). . . . We must not be too hasty in introducing ethical judgments of good and evil. Neither . . . is any less essential than the other. The phenomena of life arise from the operation of both together, whether in concert or in opposition.

—SIGMUND FREUD. In a letter to Albert Einstein in 1932 in an interchange of letters concerning delivering mankind from the menace of war.

JUST WHAT IS
THE STATE OF THE
U-N-I-O-N?

Saddening as it is to face squarely, virtually every observation points up the nearly disastrous state of most marriages.

So horrifying is the state of the union these days that, at the September, 1967, meetings of the American Psychological Association in Washington, D.C., shocking radical revisions of the whole institution of marriage were being proposed. Famed Harold Greenwald, analyst extraordinaire to the call-girl, proposed that non-legal voluntary associations be honored as marriage relationships.

> . . . Certainly those who wish it should be permitted to continue to seek the alleged security of state-certified marriage, but others not so inclined should similarly be permitted and encouraged to try alternate forms.

Similarly, a family therapist, Virginia Satir, was speaking for a marital arrangement as a "statutory five year renewable contract." The marriage contract as it stands is

> . . . potentially inhuman and anti-human and works against developing love, trust, and connectedness with other human beings. . . . Implicitly, the marriage contract abolishes individual autonomy and makes togetherness mandatory. Independent wishes and acts, contradictory opinions are seen as threats to marriage.

33

More recently, prestigious Margaret Mead wrote for the mass audience of *Life:*

> I have recommended that we have different kinds of marriages—an individual marriage in which young people who aren't ready to have children can legally live together . . . a second kind of marriage involving parental responsibility. . . . I think the longer people live and the more diverse their experience, the less likely it is that two people will stay married a lifetime. . . . We could, I believe, bring children up to accept the fact that this is a world in which divorce is a reality.

While it is quite unlikely that such suggestions will find ready or legal acceptance or that many mental-health authorities would necessarily favor them at this point, the fact is they are responsible calls for correction of a deeply troubled foundation of our entire way of life.

Let us follow the trail of evidence to how the state of the union ails so. First, consider the incredibly high divorce rate in our country. Then add the many couples who separate bitterly for periods of a time when their conflicts reach unbearable proportions; also add the couples where one spouse actually deserts the other—and often their children. In terms of firm statistics, we have data for the divorce rate that attest, most recently, to one out of three marriages breaking up! It is hard to know just what the rate becomes when we add all those couples who do not become part of the divorce statistics but who separate from each other for a period of time or who desert one another, but one gains the impression that fairly large numbers are involved.

Next, we should add the widespread phenomenon of chronic infidelity—not the occasional symptomatic or exploratory act of infidelity that we have learned is unbelievably common, nor those extramarital relationships that meet the criteria posed by some quite responsible writers for occasional, healthy mutual dalliances (whether or not we are in agreement with such a point of view), but rather marriages where one or both partners surrender to a fairly continuous pattern of subterfuge and cheating.

How high is our percentage now? Considerable. But we are still not done. Let us now add all those people who don't actually desert or play around promiscuously, but who we might discover wish passionately for any or all of these solutions to their marriages, not just occasionally, but frequently and deeply and with real strain and emotional crisis; where one or both partners are so suffused with their rage at each other that they live on their fantasies and wishes for the acting out they will not allow themselves, sometimes for deep moral reasons and courageously, sometimes out of cowardice, and sometimes out of a mixture of conviction and fear.

Finally, let us add other couples who we discover are experiencing a chronic sense of dissatisfaction with each other through much or nearly all of their married lives though they are far from chronic conscious wishes to be free of one another, but rather go on from day to day, sad or distant or chronically nagging in an essentially unknowing state of resignation to what is.

How large a figure now?

Actually, we still have not included all evidences of serious marital strain. Note, for example, other symptoms on the list offered by psychiatrist, Nathan Ackerman, a well-known authority on family therapy, as he discusses just how widespread are indications of instability of marriage in our culture:

> . . . the teenage marriage, . . . multiple marriages, loosening of sex standards, the war between the sexes, "momism," the weakness of fathers, reduction of parental authority, the broken home, emotionally injured children, the anarchy of youth, and a trend toward delinquency. With all these problems comes a growing disillusionment with the tradition and sentiment of marriage and family.

Note that Dr. Ackerman has led us from direct symptoms of strain in the marriage partners to a beginning list of problems in children of the marriage. It certainly is a near-universal experience in child-guidance work—and well do we know how busy are our child guidance practitioners—that overt and more often covert disturbance in the marriage is found to be playing a huge role in symptom consolidation in the child.

Indeed, with our increasing understanding of emotional disturbances not only as statements of the weaknesses with which people move into life from their own childhoods but as interactional responses in their current key family relationships, we now think of so many symptoms of mental illness in adults—psychosis, alcoholism—and so many symptoms of disturbance on other levels—such as psychosomatic problems and acute neurosis—as referable in significant part to a strain, often covert, in the marital relationship of the patient.

If it weren't for the fact that there are any number of hapless human beings and families who claim more than their share of several of these various symptoms of deep trouble in the marriage, it would sound as if our percentages of serious marital problems had swelled far beyond 100!

Somewhere there must indeed be some couples who are quite happy. Aren't there?

Unhappily, here too beware! At least some instances where there is apparently great happiness or contentment with the marriage—"We never fight at all, we're very happy with each other"—turn out to accompany quite serious disorders in one or another member of the family. In recent years, more sophisticated clinical understanding of such serious mental illness as schizophrenia, and such widespread and often quite serious childhood problems as psychologically based learning disorders, has shown that these very reports of good marriages may mask the inability of the couple to bear living out their natural differences with each other. We now have a term for situations where a couple unconsciously work together to sweep under the rug their various disagreements and antagonisms so as to dovetail with each other in a seemingly smooth-flowing way that wipes out the experiencing of problems and, more importantly, the experiencing of separate individuality; we call this *pseudomutuality*.

I remember, for example, at a residential treatment center for very disturbed children, two attractive young parents bringing their terribly psychotic little girl to the hospital, strolling oh-so-love-birdy down the campus, holding hands, at a time most of us would have been wringing our hands and pulling out hair at the tragedy of having to bring our child to a mental hospital.

The English psychiatrist, H. V. Dicks, reporting on a lifetime of study of marriage problems, observes about such marriages:

> There develop what might be called a collusive or joint resistance to change, a smooth facade of "happiness," of perpetual sunshine without a shadow. . . . Tensions . . . often by-pass the marital inter-action, but may break surface either in psycho-somatic form; or as periodic depression; or else they appear as neurotic problems in the children, whose unconscious cannot be cheated. Such marriages are often the envy of neighbours: placid, reasonable, and considerate. . . . When it occurs, the breakthrough of the repressed is, in such brittle unions, often a rather tragically destructive event.

Another kind of perfect marriage that has long been easily recognized by all of us as unhealthy is the doormat marriage, in which one partner never complains of his or her plight but oh-so-stolidly-and-stoicly takes whatever punishment is dished out.

With learning-disordered children, we often find that the family psychology is one in which family members have stopped learning how to grow out of their differences and conflicts, and that at least one important aspect of the child's inability to learn is that he is not free to experience aggressiveness, separateness, conflict, and differences, and accordingly must give up being able to be a creative participant in the business of exploring life.

The truth is that in attempting to understand the marital union we are into such a terribly complicated process that even expressions of happiness or unhappiness on the part of spouses are a limited index at best. In the recent *Handbook of Marriage and the Family*, sociologist Jessie Bernard concludes on this point:

> It should not be assumed that happiness in marriage means an absence of adjustment problems. In one study, it was found that although fewer of those who reported their marriage as happy needed to report personal problems in their marriage—as expected—still, even a third of the very happy marriages reported problems, and half of the above-average marriages did. Feelings of happiness in a marriage, in brief, did not mean that there were not adjustment problems present; or, conversely, the presence of adjustment problems did not necessarily militate against the happiness of the spouses.

Now, quite finally (but to this writer more important than all the possible statistics of direct and indirect indications of just how widespread, and virtually universal, are problems in marriage), is the following consideration about the nature of man: Not only do we tend to ignore the truth that virtually all marriages are deeply disturbed—and I might as well begin explaining now that to me this really means that inherently marriage is a disturbingly difficult state—but even more do we ignore the fact that *at this stage of evolution being a human being is to be an inherently disturbed and terribly incomplete creature who more often than not is suffused with destructiveness that he does not know how to handle.*

How many people know the statistic that puts all statistics of marriage disturbance to shame: that between the years 1820 and 1945, 54,000,000 human beings perished violently at the hands of their fellow human beings?

We go through life forgetting as it were that the fate of so many of our ancestors was, and the probable tragic fate of so many of us and our children may be, to die violently at the hand of other human beings. Is it little wonder then that these same *murdering homo sapiens* are so often disturbed when they are playing the role of *marrying homo sapiens?* It is the same *man*, in his primitive state of development, who enters into matrimonial union with another human being.

CHAPTER TWO

THE TRADITIONAL

MENTAL-HEALTH CONCEPT OF

MARITAL MATURITY

In the light of the consideration that the actual state of
most marriages is overtly disturbed and the sheer weight of
evidence that man as an animal is inherently disturbed, it is
surprising to find that our mental-health field too participates
in espousing the myth that although there are *many* disordered
marriages in this world of many immature people, yet the
Garden of Eden does await those mature people who do
learn how to do one or several such things as communicate
with each other *constructively* at times of conflict; match roles
appropriately; avoid clashing games in the Eric Berne sense;
analyze out and work through tendencies to regressive behavior; enjoy each other as "mature object choices" rather than
as "oedipal objects" or objects of an earlier childhood dream.

In other words, mature, healthy, or good people are to
have good marriages.

But are they?

I believe Peace Corps director, Jack Vaughn, was trying to
make a similar point regarding the illusion that peace is con-
flict-free. Speaking at a banquet inaugurating the Center for
the Study of the Causes of War and Conditions for Peace at
Utah State University, he noted:

Peace also has had its lexicon. Peace was GOOD FOR
YOU . . . the warmth and healing of sunshine . . . calm
and normalcy. . . . Paired off, "war" and "peace" were an

expression of total contrast. No blendings here . . . no confusion. Life and death. Black and white. Good and bad. War and peace. . . . Examine mercilessly, and I believe you will discover that history's favorite absolutes—"war" and "peace"—are a tragic masquerade. . . .

In effect, the mental-health field enters into the standing myth of our culture where, although just below the surface most people are aware of the tremendous disturbance in marriage, nonetheless, most people in our culture go on from day to day ignoring or suppressing this horrifying awareness and maintaining a mythology which goes something like this:

In good marriages people experience *some* differences and *even* argue once in awhile, but rarely if ever do these arguments border on the irrational or excite violently hostile passions; should this be the case, then the marriage is a disturbed marriage, and the disturbed people should get help for their problems.

Too often our mental-health world's explanations of how we end up "earning" one or another of the hells and disasters of intimacy smack of new-fangled variations on a concept of sin. It is ironic and saddening how quickly we scientists of mental health too develop priestly versions of how men suffer because they do not know our gods. Recently, I heard an otherwise profoundly innovative family therapist claim that one's emotional health should survive even a Nazi Germany if the family unit were *really* healthy!

Not that it isn't our field that helped man move centuries forward from an earlier, more blanket image of sin as *the* cause of all illness, weakness, and bad fortune. Though note that, even earlier, man had observed that all too often it really wasn't that way at all—that often terrible suffering befell the righteous who followed their god's dictates, while ostensibly evil men lived off the fat of the land.

Enter the modern era of mental-health science, and we find explanations of bad fortune, including family emotional traumas, offered in terms of individual and family psychopathology—certainly far more sophisticated statements of how men bring trouble on themselves, often unconsciously and unwittingly.

Recent work in settings such as the child-guidance field has led us to an even greater measure of acceptance of the situational or random and happenstance determinants of family disturbance, e.g., a mounting state of stress owing to illness, or death, or economic pressures, frequently crazy combinations of stresses (and particularly where the stress pattern picks up on available unconscious conflict areas and weaknesses), and before long perfectly *good* people, and people not *really* that *sick,* are roaring bitches to some spouse, or child, or family group.

Fritz Redl recently described how demoralization and decay of the larger community or nation play a role in stimulating and releasing hostility and rage in intimate relationships that would otherwise not have emerged on so destructive a scale. We have come and are coming apace from the orthodoxy that if you get into trouble, it must be because in truth *you* are, albeit unconsciously, *sick.*

All of which says that our mental-health approach to marriage is not entirely so simplistic as to divide the world into saints with altogether good marriages and sinners who are always getting too angry at each other. Over recent years there has been truly impressive growth in the sophistication of our mental-health concepts for understanding the interaction of couples.

A good example of a sophisticated contemporary statement of the mental health approach to marriage counseling is that of Emily Mudd and Hilda Goodwin of the well known Marriage Council affiliated with the Department of Psychiatry at the University of Pennsylvania:

We recognize that the choice of marital partner may represent the convergence of many different motivations, some conscious and some on a preconscious or unconscious level, that each takes into marriage some unresolved conflicts and needs or fails to meet them in ways to which the individual has been accustomed, conflicts develop, and a destructive spiral may be set in motion. This spiral leads to frustration and resentment, with a breakdown in meaningful communication. It enhances failure to support each partner's personal identity, and as a result fails to alleviate anxiety about oneself and the threatened loss of the marriage.

It is clear that the child in all of us is recognized by these counselors; but, still, notice the prevailing myth they support: most couples make it, but *some* poor souls get in trouble.

Let it be entirely clear that there is indeed something decisively important about communication in marriage. One study after another has shown that happier marriages involve far more sharing of events, and feelings, also far fewer turnings off of communication when problems arise. The trouble is that most talk of communication between spouses sounds like a Robert (*Father Knows Best*) Young prescription for calm, friendly sharing of differences between spouses, and few of us mortals are equal to such.

In recent years we have also had some greater recognition that a good deal of regressive behavior takes place quite naturally within all marriages. University of Pennsylvania sociologist, Otto Pollak, speaks of "nonpathological regression" and the ways in which each partner is called on to accept and/or assist his spouse to restrict the extent of his nonpathological regression. Before the arrival of children, the marriage partners are to free each other to use their marriage to play out some such regression; but then over the course of childrearing, one of the roles of each partner is to assist the other to inhibit the regression in the presence of the children. Note, however, the tour de force of defining acceptable regression as "nonpathological"; without a definition of just what this means, we are still left with largely the same framework that anything that looks pretty wild is necessarily pathological.

Pollak has also come very close to identifying the inevitability of conflict between spouses as being not because of anger or emotional immaturity but because of two people being two people.

> One person, without any hostility, aggression, or intent to hurt—merely through the expression of his existence—may be damaging for another.

However, here too Pollak strains to keep conflict within the realm of pathology by accounting for the natural conflict as an expression of "developmental arrest . . . on different levels" in the two partners, for example, "an oral character in the wife and an anal character in the husband."

Another important dimension of our increasing sophistication in analyzing marriage difficulties has been the growth of our understanding of just how deep and intimate is the tie between most partners—including marriages where there is ostensibly nothing but a mutual well of hate, and including marriages where one of the partners is ailing with a psychological disorder while the apparently healthier spouse seemingly stands by. We have come to see both powerful reciprocity and complementarity between marriage partners. Essentially, the contemporary concept is this: Married couples tend to be quite opposite in many basic emotional traits, and disturbance in one partner is generally complemented by a similar extreme in the other direction in the partner; also, underneath these differences, married couples tend to show the same basic level of real ego strength or weakness.

A brilliant psychoanalytic clinician, Peter Giovachini, writes:

I have come to the conclusion that the nature and depth of psychopathology are identical for the husband and wife in the long-established marriage. Indeed, a marriage may be characterized by strife and turmoil and appear to be on the brink of collapse. Yet in spite of continuing misery, one senses how necessary the marriage is for each partner's psychic survival . . . the underlying personalities of the husband and wife are similar. . . . We find that their basic conflicts, their points of fixation and regression, and their general ego integrations are the same. . . .

This concept brings us somewhat closer to a broader feeling for the essential human continuity of disturbance in a marriage—for now it is not only a given disturbed person, but a similarity in the partner and a dovetailing of needs that is being played out, and we know that the ostensibly disturbed partner is generally only one of at least two people in trouble. Still, though, the contemporary myth plods on that these two are disturbed, but many other people are so much healthier.

By now, mental-health studies have also come to describe fairly vividly the process by which so many couples move from the original land of enchantment to progressive disillusionment and marriage agonies. A particularly simple and clear description of this process is given by family therapist, Virginia Satir. She describes how a Mary and a Joe decide to marry. They risk relating to each other despite all their fears because they are at a point where their sexual passions have come to the fore, and also because at that point their love for each other makes each feel that if only there were a permanent union each would enjoy a continuing sense of completeness. Both end up living for each other. They enter into a "survival pact." Satir writes:

Each said privately to himself: "If I run out of supplies, I will take from you. You will have enough, in an emergency, to serve us both." After marriage though, Mary and Joe discover that they are different in ways which seem to take away rather than add to them, and now they are forever reminded that each is not an extension of the other, who completes him, but a separate being.

Why do Joe and Mary get stuck? Because of their original poor self-esteem. Had they had good self-esteem, they would not have written such a bogus contract for completeness with one another is the implication; were they capable of better self-esteem, they would not fall prey to the disillusioned discovery that neither can afford to complete the other.

Each would feel confident in his ability to get from the other. Each could even wait to get. Each could give to the other without himself feeling robbed. Each could use the differentness of the other as an opportunity for growth.

All of which is a beautiful description of a process of demoralization on the one hand and of a mature ideal on the other. However, at least in this description in what was a 1964 publication, Satir did not seem to take into account the reality that most young people go into marriage at a point where their self-esteem is quite shaky or at least immature, and therefore that virtually all marriages go through the cycle she describes so well. Granted the Joe and Mary who are especially weak in self-esteem beforehand are *really* in for trouble in marriage, but isn't everybody else too? Consider Mrs. Satir's more recent proposal for a five-year renewable marriage contract; she apparently agrees things are rough for all of us Joes and Marys.

Closer to conceptualizing the universality of marital disorder are those forward thinkers in mental health who see all human beings as inherently emotionally vulnerable. Thus, Lawrence Kubie, in a contribution to an important collection of papers on marital problems, wrote:

At the present point in the evolution of human culture a neurotic process is universal.

The recent book by English psychiatrist, Dicks, to which we referred earlier, has provided a breathtaking analysis of marital tensions based on object-connection concepts of personality development, where areas of one's traumatic experiences are split off from the central ego; then, in marital interaction there is a powerful interplay between the system of each partner, especially in the way of projection onto one another of those very split-off qualities in oneself that are so feared.

Insofar as Dicks has penetrated to universal issues in the underworld of personality structure in his analysis of marital difficulties, one senses and infers that he is indeed talking about all of us and our spouses to one extent or another. However, when he surfaces to discuss concretely the marriage-problem clientele and the professional roles of helpers, we are disappointed to find again various qualities of a sick versus healthy categorization.

It is hard to let go of the picture of Marriage Beautiful and Serene that we would hope for!

CHAPTER THREE

THE UNDERLYING MYTH

OF HAPPY FAMILY LIFE

Underlying the mythology of Happy Marriage for the Well Adjusted, there is a deeper myth yet that involves all of us, children along with grownups.

This is the myth of Happy Family Life Awaiting Him Who Is Good, Decent, Fair, Well Analyzed, Self-Actualized, or What Have You.

We teach our children to believe and hope that if they are "good"—translate for a more sophisticated contemporary mental-health version: "if they work hard at their family relationships"—their family lives *should* be decent, fair, healthy, rewarding, even joyous.

But the reality of life is entirely different—for all of us. Children and adults encounter, at every stage of family life, injustice and bitter betrayal of their most cherished relationships.

On what basis do we propose this disheartening generalization?

With no little heaviness of heart and with a fearful sense of unreality about it all, I venture to say: "On the basis of observation of myself, my family, my patients, my colleagues, and my friends; and then, in turn, of all their observations of other people."

Over and over again we see not only disturbed marriages, described earlier, and not only many emotionally disturbed adults and children traceable to the marriage problems, but also, significant in their own right, such tragic travesties on happy family life as these:

Mothers who reject, hate, and persecute their children

Fathers who abandon, resent, or ignore—and impotently resign their children and wives to each other while pretending loyalty to both

Siblings who turn on each other and away from each other —and in later adult years can not even bear to know each other

Children who resist, mock, and attack their mortal parents' offers of caring

Family systems that systematically maintain a scapegoat to carry the burden of pain, rage, and weakness of other seemingly strong family members

Children who become mocking devil-figures of precisely that which was coveted but feared and expelled from their family lives

Sabotage and revolutions against family codes of all sorts —in social behavior, marital or vocational choice, ideological identification, choice of residence . . .

And on and on . . .

And here, again, we take a leap to feeling about the larger, infinitely more bizarre record of man's injustices to man in persecutions and wars, and death camps of all sorts—and then we return to conclude regarding family life that these same men could not possibly have felt from their own families *as* deep and abiding a respect for their own lives as we should like to take for granted in ordinary human events where people are reasonably caring toward each other. Nor could they feel such for their children, and wives, and parents, if they could serve so readily as executioners or accomplices to executioners.

Yet, the Myth of Happy Family Life persists, often aided and abetted by our own field of mental health.

So much of our thinking about human troubles still seeks to remove universal existential or experiential dilemmas to a world of *pathology*, or to conceive of problems as states of *disorder* or, worst of all, to see failures of human spirit as statements of intrinsic *incompetence*.

And the basic message of the mental-health field to human beings is that Virtue Rewarded, the Faithful may indeed live stress-free lives, if only they believe and yield reverently in the Temple of Psychotherapy to work through their individual and family psychopathological wills to fail.

It is then a bitter discovery to learn how numerous are the analysands, and other seekers of the faith, and, yes, our analysts and all we teachers of the faith, who in truth reap harvests of hate in their family lives.

Someday—soon, I would hope—we need to have fuller Gallup, Kinsey, and Mid-Town Metropolis* types of data about what really happens to people in family life; and, yes, we would recommend beginning with a down-to-earth study of the family lives of those of us who are the therapists and counselors of our fellowmen and their families!

What then is the last recourse "when prophecy fails"—a frequent situation in man's history of trying ever so beautifully and ever so rigidly to put a final order to his universe? In our mental-health world, we fall back on our variants of explanations of heresy: There was resistance to treatment or a failure to experience in a real way the inner meanings of the issues considered in therapy, or treatment was insufficient to

---

* This is the study conducted in a midtown section of Manhattan where it was found that 80% to 90% or more of the population were suffering from symptoms generally taken by mental-health people as indicative of emotional disturbance! A compelling truth, but one that the mental-health field has been hard-pressed to deal with as long as the sick-healthy distinction remains the key working concept of diagnosis rather than concepts of personal and collective evolution. When we ask how far has man come along in his potential for mental health and family fun, we are much freer to be honest about the terrible agonies of most families than if we have to end up saying everyone is sick, sick.

begin with—all so often entirely true, but not at all always true, and in many cases so ludicrously reminiscent of the dodges and automatic defenses to be found in every doctrinal group from time immemorial.

What is rarely conceived is that family injustices and betrayals are a function of the inherent humanness of us all, as a statement of many qualities intrinsic to man.

We need to learn to feel and stay with our episodes of crisis and demoralization, to feel our pain which must be and is the fuel of change, but also somehow at the same time to entertain a kind of existential resignation and humor, however wry, and though in a vale of otherwise quite real tears, to know that such real pains are of the essence of life's challenge.

It should be a goal of psychotherapy—an often beautifully effective process—and the goal of all education and training for the long haul of one's personal and family emotional life, to expect and accept—indeed, if it does not appear, to seek!—pain and conflict and injustice and betrayal as the stuff of life from which grow joy and becoming and love and family wholesomeness, though always in cyclical, complexly interweaving processes of growth and decay, life and death.

CHAPTER FOUR

INJUSTICE

INTRINSIC TO THE

NATURE OF MAN

Let us consider how injustice is intrinsic to the nature of man.

The simplest truth, yet one so difficult for us to comprehend about ourselves, is that we, man, live out all of our lives as a part of a nature in which there abound never-ending processes of waxing and waning, birth and death, creation and destruction.

As inhabitants of nature, we are also responsive to nature's thrusts of cataclysmic storms, or volcanos or earthquakes; yet, we also depend on the same earth and skies that rumble and overwhelm us to bring forth harvests of food. We are vulnerable to threats from a never-ending variety of colleague biological creatures—lions to eat us, snakes that would poison us, viruses that infect us; yet it is to the same myriad of biologic creatures that we also turn for food and medicine and mysterious feats of biological balance. Everywhere there are sunrises and sunbursts of beauty, and sunstorms and sunspots of hell.

Even if we were not a part of these same processes, we could not help but be responsive to them; and even if we were not responsive, in the final analysis we could not help but be observers of these models of nature all around us, and in turn model some of our styles of management of our own human affairs along similar lines.

Here then we are: nature's creatures of beauty, yet her victims too—to cancers and infections and angry seas and bitter cold and fire and whatnot. Here then we are: creators of a Man World in which *we* bring the lives of millions of us to a violent end—in gas chamber holocausts, in Biafran starvation, in brilliant atom explosions, in games called war, in crusades claiming religious nobility, and so forth.

It is really very, very difficult.

For twentieth-century man, still so suffering, there may be at least some relief in discovering that we can equip ourselves to study our own natures far more than man could dream of doing at any previous time.

Whether or not we yet understand ultimate causations of man's evil—and I believe we do not—we are in a position to understand naturalistically that much of man's never-ending cycles of injustice derive unwittingly from the very nature of man.

I would suggest that we consider at this time four intrinsic conditions in man's nature which dictate the inevitability of *aggression*—that is, the essentially natural energy stream of man, but which also underlies and easily manifests itself in a ready potential for *destructiveness*.

1. Man's basic life energy is explosive

There is a two-sidedness to so much of the nature of which we are part. The pulsating, tumultuous energy that is the motor of man's unbelievable energetic thrust for exploration, inventiveness, creation, development, and so forth can also be volatile, inflammable, incendiary, fast-spreading, feeding on itself, and explosive; if man is to utilize such energy sources effectively, he must learn to beware how inadvertently he may burn and destroy rather than fire, energize, and create. Everyone knows that playing with fire is fire!

2. Man-animal is a pecking-order, territory-apportioner, survivor-of-the-fittest, and best-male-gets-the-female creature

The story of man's use of power, and need for power, has only been written partially, in my opinion, especially in psychology.

Dominance-submission conflicts seem to characterize so many intimate and public human interactions.

And not-power-crazy people so often seem unable to restrain and modulate their strength when given power, or after having earned a position of leadership over others.

Power does corrupt, it would seem.

Man-animal seeks such power.

And having gained it, over-uses it—so often almost begging others to stop him.

We know little of how to tap the strength of these forces and to re-channel them.

3. Man is vulnerable and therefore must maintain strategic defense weaponry on a standby alert

Though there is indeed majesty in his creation, every human being is necessarily profoundly incomplete. For all that man, black and white, is beautiful black and white, each of us is also deeply vulnerable—a fragile speck of life that can be wiped out so easily. Man is therefore given to a never-ending state of concern, anxiety, and awareness of risk; and feeling vulnerable, man must rightly maintain a state of alert—or readiness for defense. Such a state of alert means that man must maintain a standby reservoir of strategic defenses and weaponry—such as anger, hate, hostility, and destructiveness. Note how none of these defenses feels intrinsically bad when seen in this way as genuine tools for self-defense.

Unfortunately, for all that man may be intending honorable defense of his person, it is a rare thing to find people who have the wisdom to gauge just how much strength to put to the fight without rushing to an overfight and overkill that in turn incite further attack from the enemy. Note how virtually every war and even genocide in the history of man has been seen by each side as a declaration of self-defense—include the Nazis; include the Turks who slaughtered the Armenian people; include the endless territorial wars or religious wars of man; and on and on. Note similarly how in family wars, such as on the marital battleground, virtually every person sincerely experiences himself as the beleaguered one fighting in self-defense. Man has a good deal to learn about how to test more objectively his overpowering convictions of being attacked—and then feeling justified to release his strategic bombers.

4. Man must fight off the very close relationships he otherwise needs in order to achieve a separate identity

From infancy, each of us is deeply, deeply dependent on the responses of another and others; and even in these early years, we also begin to feel the other side of the coin of what it means for us to be able to give something that is of value to the others, who, in their very caring for us, also are dependent on our responses for feedback validation of their being. In all of our giving and receiving, we depend on the reciprocity with another . . . and ultimately with a whole community of others.

At the same time, these same ties cannot be too close. The family group that lies down together in undue closeness may soon find themselves unable to rise to challenging calls from within, say for learning or for sexual joy, lest these pulsations—that are such great pleasures for others—intrude and disrupt the togetherness of the family-plan bedroom. Undue need for feedback signs from another that our gifts are good all too often defeats the very intent of our caring. In the animal world, we know mothers to expel their children from the nest. Perhaps in human events too, some of what may appear to us as divisive, rejecting, or destructive may be, or began as, an attempt at challenging one's child to growth for self.

The task for all of us is yet to depend on another, yet to be a source of support to this other, yet to separate from the other. Here again life faces us with a counterpointing of forces: depending, yielding, taking, enjoying, experiencing gratitude; giving, feeding, nourishing, supporting; and then too, attacking, leaving, parting, making oneself different from, posing oneself against; saying all that, yes, I come unto you, but I must be free to go from you, to come and to go, to be thine but mine.

And the natural laws for becoming one's own person deem it necessary and proper that much becomes forged through civil protest, and student rebellion, resistance movements, guerrilla raids, declarations of independence, wars of independence, all potentially decent, freedom-seeking efforts, but all so easily running amuck into anarchy and destructiveness.

How much is the inevitability of injustice recognized in existing mental-health maps of *normal* human experiences and in *normal* family life?

Certainly many observations have been made of the fact that people living together in families, or together on our planet, must experience differences; but these differences are so often pictured in a pale light of Sunday-church emotions as reasonable, cognitive alternatives which people of good will can resolve readily.

There are also many existential acknowledgments of the pain that marks man's course through life. But even much of this material seems to refer to a tough luck and to rough deals, that are somehow our lot from our gods, or from nature, or from a probabilistic Nevada fortune-wheel fate; and not so much to the fact that we are men of nature, and hence generators and parts of natural cycles of growth and decay.

We do have deeper penetrations that picture the more real

color and depth of struggle at one or another point of the normal developmental sequence.

A British pediatrician and psychiatrist, D. Winnicot, has described brilliantly the inevitable rage of a mother at her infant, for many reasons, including the fact that mother must naturally become overwhelmed by the demands of mothering, but most important because mother and infant *must* separate from one another, and anger is a vehicle of such individuation.

Incidentally, he calls to the attention of psychotherapists that the same truth obtains for us in our mothering—helping our patients.

Harvard University psychiatrist Joseph Rheingold has described the process more from the point of view of a state of disturbance in the mother—the mother who feels inadequate to her job as a provider must feel angry at her child—but he posits such disturbance is so well nigh universal that, from our point of view, he is adding to our beginning map of the naturalistic sequences of aggression in all of us. His more important contribution, we believe, is that he traces the process of how most mothers deny their rage at the child, and how the part of the child's underlying personality that is the recipient of such denied rage in turn harbors and projects rage at others.

California psychologist George Bach's contribution is well known to many Americans. In his recent trail-setting work on marital fighting (to which we will devote much greater attention later), Dr. Bach talks a good deal about couples' needs to maintain optimum distance from each other out of the underlying naturalness of all of us needing to maintain separateness. He also proposes a forthright concept of aggression in the service of one's naturalness, but then how man gets into trouble using his strength:

Man is in a chronic state of aggression-overmobilization. Each individual has, therefore, an embarrassing stockpile

of surplus aggression in readiness and he must do something constantly or periodically to release some of it. Con-
sequently, man is in a constant search for enemies who can
serve as safe aggression-release targets. All segments of a
culture (not just politicians) share in the search for and/or
invention of enemies; once found, people go after them
with hostile gusto, as history amply demonstrates. . . . The
release of aggressive impulses (like the release of sexual
impulses) should become a *personal responsibility*—being
taken care of among friends, NOT enemies.

These are some of the exciting breakthrough concepts of
our day. However, one can hardly yet conclude that a psychological science has now emerged to teach people how *our lives,
in general, and including our normal family lives, will be at-
tended by a continuous thread of tension, anger, hostility, and
unfairness that is a function not of pathology, nor of stress,
but of the core of humanness in all of us.*

The result is many of us still strive for, and are defeated by
the absence of a family life that is quiet. We therefore also fail
to learn to get the most out of yielding to our pain and to the
process of growth and change that injustice may serve.

an alternative point of view:

MARITAL MATURITY AS

LOVING AND HATING

How then might we now return specifically to look at marriage if we are indeed prepared to come to terms with the sad facts of what is going on all around us?

For those of us who would still like to think that *some day* at least *some* humans may reach the kind of peacefulness and respectful cooperation with each other that has long been our ideal image of marriage, it still would be wiser for the moment to set up a far lesser goal for most of us human beings. We would set a lesser goal for marriage on the pragmatic basis that at this point in evolution the obviously largest majority of humans cannot approach the ideal. This point of view would be very much consistent with the startling finding we referred to earlier and that so many people have found hard to assimilate, that epidemiological study has shown that if you really count heads and noses from the point of view of traditional psychiatric concepts of illness, the largest part of the population—as much as 80 to 90 percent—show up as starkly emotionally disordered. So, strictly from a practical point of view, let us be wise enough to leave it that for the next few hundred years, maybe a few thousand years, we shall say to people that they should expect in their marriages an awful lot of rough spots and much, much anger, but what they should try to do is to learn *how* to argue with each other without beating each other's brains in, and how not to take their upsets that seriously that they upset themselves twice as much.

For those of us who are prepared to go even further to give up the ideal of mature marital cooperation as so remote from the immediate potential of the human race as to be more detrimental than helpful; and for those of us who are prepared to consider that it may be inevitable in our humanness that we all experience so much aggressiveness and anger that inevitably marriages are going to be shaky sharings of differences and anger between people, there is an even more direct route to changing our concept of the goal of marital maturity.

What we say is that there must always be a fairly high level of tension, dissension, anger, conflict, also irrationality, and unfairness between couples (nice guys finish last and all that); but that the trick of the *reasonably* working marriage is to learn such things as how to tap the energy of these fights for stimulating better efforts in each spouse; how to feel anger at each other, but to learn never to translate these feelings into overt reactions such as overt physical attacks against another's person; how to silently enjoy the thrust of anger in one's partner—even as the partner makes you madder than hell—as an expression of the other's life force seeking to assert itself which, quietly honored, without excessive retaliation, may lead to the development of a stronger and healthier partner whom one can enjoy somewhat more.

From our point of view, then, the way of assuring many more marriages going on the rocks, or getting bogged down in chronic misery, is to keep shooting for marriages in which there is no misery; to keep offering people marriage ceremonials in which they are enjoined to love, honor, and obey each other; to compromise with each other; to empathize more for the other than for oneself; and so forth. We say that the marriage ceremony might better caution people that in truth it is inevitable that their marriage will be filled with misery and anger, and that it is their adult jobs to learn to love and hate, to honor and dishonor, obey and disobey in the best balanced way that they can achieve.

The adult who wishes to be effective in marriage—for his own sake, let alone "for the children" (real caring for one's kids is the extension of one's real caring for oneself), and last still out of respect for his spouse (though there is maturity in such interpersonal commitment too)—such an adult should be prepared for the inevitability that he will want "out" from his marriage; that his pain will be deep and many of his grievances against his spouse quite "real"; and yet that the trick for enjoying the pleasures of marriage is to commit oneself to working at the inevitable troubles, working hard and ingeniously at the union with all of its attendant limitations.

Not to be overwhelmed or too sorry for oneself when the marriage crisis comes is half the battle.

By yielding to the inevitable misery and anger in marriage, just as by yielding to the inevitability of storms as a feature of nature, or to the inevitability of sickness in the biological history of man, or to the inevitability of death as the end point of all human life, we may have a somewhat greater opportunity to be happy, or at least to learn not to be thrown quite so much by our unhappiness as we are so long as we hold on to our current make-believe that *we* have gotten stuck with a dirty deal because we are miserable with our spouse.

To offer oneself and one's spouse the security of a commitment to brave the challenge of the marriage, if at all possible, is much of the other half of the battle.

And then there may come a surprising discovery: The capacity to stay with one's marital trials in itself frees and stimulates a deep process of possible further personal growth and self renewal to find more real meaning and value in oneself, as the real source of one's life pleasure and security since our so-aggravating spouse (and it would be the same with any other spouse!) falls so short of making us feel as good as we once believed we would deserve and require of another.

Martin Grotjahn, a brilliant student of the family neurosis

as an extended representation of the unconscious of each partner, observes:

> The potentialities for working through in marriage are also the best defense of monogamy. The monogamous relationship is a life-long pressure for working through and not avoiding it.

No matter what, one must expect marriages to face crises of growth; spouses should prepare to have what Rudolf Dreikurs has called so beautifully,

> the courage to let themselves be pulled down by the whirlpool of life and be spilled out safely.

CHAPTER SIX

AGGRESSIVENESS

AS A CONSTRUCTIVE FORCE

IN MARRIAGE AND IN LIFE

So far, we have been reluctantly yielding to the fact of aggressiveness as a sadly inescapable quality of existence. However, the fact is that there are some aspects of aggressiveness that are really quite positive. We tend to forget these because so often aggressiveness ends up in destructive expressions that are so devastating that we naturally fear the very sources of such power without realizing that much aggressiveness can be constructive in its nature.

Thus, L.A. Coser, a sociologist, has pointed out how, from a larger point of view of social organization, aggression plays at least three positive roles: as a form of achievement such as when committed to revolutions against oppression; as a danger signal calling for much needed change (a good example in our own time would be the demonstrations of American Blacks); and as a catalyst of social change.

In biological life, we have learned that aggression plays key *life-serving* roles in survival of the fittest (the basic Darwinian concept, of course); also for spacing out or apportioning territory to the species; also as a tonic for the stimulation and effecting of the whole symphony of drives; and even as a basis for the evolution of a bond of affiliativeness—and love.

This last function of aggression is especially remarkable for our purposes. It is fantastic to see that only among those animals who show significant aggression within their species does there also evolve a love-bonding; that without hating-killing there is no emerging counterpoint of loving. Shades of human lovers!

In psychological affairs, too, we have increasing evidence of the significance of aggressiveness as a life force; its absence marks weakness, lack of energy for projecting oneself, lack of stamina for creativity, lack of zest for recovery from emotional problems.

Aggressiveness is the hum of life, the spirit of being.

This has long been understood in popular, instinctive psychology: We are forever curiously gauging another man's real strength by the vitality of his bearing and manner. In projective test-studies of people, we look for indications of drive and affect strength.

In treatment of various serious emotional disorders and mental illness, we find so often not only an excess of anger that is burning up the person himself, but an excess that in many ways is built on a base of improper release or utilization of the natural aggression one needs for successful living. Much of the treatment process is intended to teach people how to feel anger, and share their anger with their family and associates without fearing that their anger will in fact destroy another.

In treatment of various sexual disorders, we frequently find fear of one's aggression inhibiting the flow of sexual vigor; in treatment, an effort is made to help people be angry at the very person they love and desire; also, on another level, to be physically penetrating and vigorous toward their sexual partner.

This last point is particularly significant for our consideration of the marital relationship. For it reminds us that in the cornerstone area of the basic sexual contract of marriage there is to be a never-ending aggressiveness—a never-ending fusion of anger with loving feeling. It is surprising that we have been so long in coming to an extrapolation of this principle to the broader range of the marital relationship; that the couple who can hate each other *and* love each other may stay together, with some real satisfaction no less, for all that they too must indeed endure many painful low points and troubling unsure experiences of bitterness with each other.

Let us consider specifically some of the positive values of aggressiveness in the marital union:

1. Our spouse is a colleague, critic, teacher, and supervisor.

It is good for us human beings to be able to share our differences with a colleague; it is good for each of us to have the feedback of just-right-after-opening-night criticisms of our productions, also more sober, long-after review; it is good to have the opportunity to learn different ideas from others, and to enjoy a measure of supervision of our work.

2. Our spouse is a reacting, stimulating, catalyzing force.

It is good for human beings to function in an atmosphere in which there is fairly continuous stimulation, even irritation, or provocation to achieving even more, rather than resting on one's laurels too smugly.

3. From what we know of the structure of marriages, given the particular characteristic of most marital unions as involving people who differ quite dramatically on certain key psychological characteristics, there is the possibility of each partner teaching the other those qualities in which the one partner is quite strong and in which the second partner is particularly weak.

A simple example is the fair young maid, socially more comfortable and winning, who may be able to bolster the shakier, more socially withdrawing man to dare experiment with becoming more winning socially. Since the op-

positeness of people often also implies a degree of extreme-
ness even on the part of the mate who seems blessed with
the more positive side of a trait, conflict between spouses
may also help reduce the too-good extreme. Thus, the so-
ciable lady may also be a person who is too driven to so-
cialize; and in conflict with a mate who tends to be more
withdrawn but also possibly more given to inner depth,
she may learn to quiet down, and search for more inner
value in her interpersonal relationships.

4. An even more subtle but we believe important point
about the oppositeness of marriage partners is that by and
large we know that underneath whatever extreme is represented in the overt stance of a human being, there is so often
an unconscious oppositeness in that person himself. In the
conflicting interchange between mates, there is also a struggle
around these unconscious opposites, and hopefully, if the marriage struggle moves along constructively, there is also change
developing on this level of the secret emotional understructure
of each spouse.

> For example, take the generally fair mate and the charac-
> teristically unfair mate in fights. The one generally seeks
> to pacify and to be reasonable. The other generally attacks
> and carries on as an unrelenting "hawk." Yet, often we
> find deep in the hawk considerable fairness and sensitivity;
> and in the fairer, more righteous mate, so often under-
> neath hugely vindictive, unreasonable anger.

5. There is often value in a clash of forces insofar as it
creates energy.

> We now take for granted the miraculous physics of elec-
> trical potential as it involves plus and minus elements. So
> too may it be that the interplay of complementary qualities
> within us as individuals produces the energy of a search

for a balanced expression of ourselves. And so too does the clash of various levels of difference and oppositeness between peoples such as a couple in marriage produce energy, vitality, zest, and power for life, for them and for their children stimulated by this environment.

Needless to say, if the wires are uninsulated, or if you're standing in a puddle when you touch the hot wire, or if you do any of the other kinds of things that are wrong when you're dealing with electricity, you can burn yourself up! But if you learn to tap the energy, wire it, channel it appropriately to its goal-points for activating other machinery, and create on and off switches, circuit breakers, dimmers and whatnot, then there is the possibility of getting to a more creative state precisely because you do have power machinery working for you, and not just your own old handtools!

CHAPTER SEVEN

THE CRISIS OF FAMILY INJUSTICE

Let us follow a typical sequence of a person's hurt and anger in a family crisis:

How could you do this to me?

> *I don't know if I can survive!*
> *Am I really capable of living through such hurt?*

I HATE YOU!!

> *The pain is unbearable! I can't stand it!!*
> *I don't know what to do!!*

Destructive Alternative A:

You deserve everything I do to you!

I am going to give you back worse!

I am going to . . . !

Destructive Alternative B:

I can't stand the pain of what you have done to me!

I wish I were dead!

*I'll show you just how much you've hurt me,
and then you'll be sorry!*

NO!

I can't really do it!

Neither!

   I can't go off half-cocked, either against you or against me, because

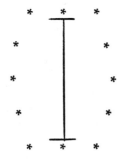

   really deserve better

(than either of those alternatives would show me to be)!

My God

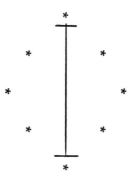

am more valuable!

I do deserve better no matter what you or anybody else does to me!

I will love myself despite you, you son-of-a bitch!

I do hate you!

But now, somehow, I also understand how driven you feel!

Somehow, I don't hate you as much!

In fact, I appreciate how you are trying . . . !

It is no wonder that so many people seek to avoid such crisis. The pain *is* near unbearable.

Most of all, it is the pain of one's own worst self-regard!

It is also the devastating fear of one's own intense rage— and fear of destroying all around us, including ourselves!

And it is fear of loss of our loved ones!

There is no one!

Yet there is me!

Much of this process has been described quite fully in many observations from time immemorial of how so many individuals are brought to a state of crisis in their lives.

There is Biblical Job.

There is twentieth-century psychoanalysis as a technique for inducing a state of crisis at the deepest personality level.

There is Zen as another-culture way of also bringing people to an unbearable state of pain—to precede the fulfillment, letting-go miracle of the *satori* experience of wholeness— vigorousness—peace.

But we have not seen this individual-crisis sequence as part and parcel of the family process too.

We do have help from psychologist Albert Ellis and his colleague "rational-emotive therapists" who teach us so clearly and simply that if someone else calls us inadequate, our hurt and anger are based on our own confirming thought; within ourselves, we are saying, "Yes, I am inadequate." One must learn how to say inside, "I don't need to think of myself as inadequate or unlovable just because the other regards me so."

This seemingly simple tour de force is enormously important!

But the natural process of family injustice demands something more: You can't beat the rap to the point of missing the pain to begin with! Before one can reach the conviction not to beat his own brains in, one must first live through a good measure of the pain which forces the confrontation to begin with. And this is hard!

We also honor in particular the pioneering contributions of family therapy to the management of crisis through confrontation and authentic communication and (especially, fair) fighting with one's family bedevilers.

There is enormous relief and repair possible when one tells one's pain and anger *like it is* to the other(s).

And in the next chapters we will be looking at specific principles of such communication to our spouse in marital fighting.

However, not only is it hard to get to such communicating, and to do it right in the heat of family crisis, but ultimately there is a piece of the sequence of family injustice that will admit no interpersonal solution, and which must be played out only in what one does inside of one's own heart of feelings for oneself.

The kinds of behaviors that family members choose as the vehicles for their challenges are by no means simple; they include potentially lethal sticks and stones that might break my bones; let alone when kept to words, the attack from a loved one is not in trivial words that can never hurt me: the attacks are real life displays of coldness, rejection, rudeness, unfairness, lack of understanding, sexual treachery, betrayal to friends or associates, public humiliation, and what not—all of which will bring any of us strong humans to feel idiotically weak before we can begin to search for the possibility of reaffirming our value despite these insults to us that echo the part-despair and empty center that exists in all of us.

Here too let us leap to the bigger world of chimney hell where surviving man must face an incomparable despair about other human beings. Richard Rubinstein, a rabbi who identifies himself with the concept "God is dead," writes in *After Auschwitz:*

> We have learned in the crisis that we were totally and nakedly alone, that we could expect neither support nor

succor from God or from our fellow creatures. . . . We have lost all hope and faith. We have also lost all possibility of disappointment. Expecting absolutely nothing from God or man, we rejoice in whatever we receive. . . . We accept our nothingness—nay, we even rejoice in it—for in finding our nothingness, we have found both ourselves and the God who alone is true substance.

In family life, those who will yet persist and do succeed in discovering themselves despite the wrongness of the Other may in turn stimulate and release the Other to discover their also-goodness despite the role they have just played in being attackers and hurters.

In effect, self-acceptance in such crisis cuts the circle of aggression and counter-aggression; and introduces a theme or motif of individual decency, despite the action of the Other which cannot really do me in, that also offers the other party an opportunity for clearer perception of the good in them, and of their destructiveness as no-longer necessary in defense against the destructiveness of another, us!

And it is often out of arriving at such self-acceptance that one is freer to enter into the very kinds of family therapy and communication that do indeed provide vehicles for release of anger and *quid pro quos* and forgiveness and recommitment.

CHAPTER EIGHT

MARRIAGE COUNSELING OR TREATMENT:

TEACHING PEOPLE TO EXPECT DIFFICULTY

AND TO LEARN

HOW TO FIGHT EACH OTHER

CONSTRUCTIVELY

We come then to the conclusion that it is not only important for couples to revise the marriage contract, but it is important for mental-health practitioners to revise the offer of help they extend.

A few clinicians have recognized that we need to teach troubled marriage partners a lot more of how to live with their spouse's limitations rather than forever stimulate self-righteous anger over a spouse's neurosis or infantile conflicts or what have you. (So often the hollow sad sounds of justification for divorce ring with these somehow-not-true-truths about a partner one was compelled to leave.)

For some, the point is made indirectly. Albert Ellis and his associates who work from the point of view of rational-emotive psychotherapy (whom we cited a little while ago as teaching how not to say *to oneself* what the "enemy" is saying to us) emphasize such considerations as never surrendering to blaming another person for one's misery—it is fruitless and only adds to the trouble. They also emphasize not needing to be perfect all the time. Most of all they emphasize not being that concerned with one's social appearance, and in this respect, as applied to marriage trouble, they do help a great deal in taking the sting out of so many marital problems where it is not only that people feel miserable that they're getting such a raw deal if they find themselves needing to fight with one another, but that they are also afraid of being exposed socially. The result of such concern is generally misery that is increased many times over what it is to begin with in its own right.

More direct awareness of the inevitability of conflict, and even the desirability of conflict in marriage has been expressed by only relatively few psychotherapeutic writers. Interestingly enough, many of these have appeared in one specific setting, a recent exciting departure in scientific journalism, the journal of the American Academy of Psychotherapists, *Voices: The Art and Science of Psychotherapy*, which emphasizes a more honest sharing of therapists' own feelings, a freer style of writing with less stylized scientifism, and yet a continuing drawing on the root springs of science.

In an exciting issue devoted to the theme of hate and aggression, the editors of the journal, John Warkentin and Tom Leland, dedicate the issue to "the Struggle, that of the therapist with his patient, that of the husband and wife, that of the parent and child, and to the struggle which we each have with ourselves."

In an extraordinarily pioneering paper elsewhere, one of the editors, Dr. Warkentin, collaborating with Carl Whitaker, points out how the usual rules of social behavior do not apply to marriage:

Fairness is not appropriate . . . consistency is impossible . . . decency, face-saving, and factual honesty are all of minor significance in marriage.

In another issue of *Voices* devoted specifically to marriage, we find a parable of marriage by Allen Wheelis whose professional writings mark him as an undoubtedly fine psychoanalyst, and who also has the distinction of being a novelist who had the courage in a first novel to portray a psychoanalyst who achieves large professional heights while all the time he is playing a deeply destructive role in his own family. In his parable, he writes of Henry and Lorabelle who suffered oh-all-the-bitter-ups-and-downs-of-marriage. Finally, they came to some measure of effective loving:

Henry and Lorabelle loved each other most of the time, tried to love each other all the time, to create a pure bond, but could not. It was marred by the viciousness, shocking to them, with which they hurt each other. Out of nothing they would create fights, would yell at each other, hate, withdraw finally in bitter silent armistice; then, after a few hours, or sometimes a few days, would come together again with some final smashes and skirmishes, and try to work things out—to explain, protest, forgive, understand, forget, and above all to compromise. It was a terribly painful and always uncertain process; and even while it was under way Henry would think bleakly, "It won't last, will never last; we'll get through this one maybe, probably, then all will be well for a while—a few hours, days, weeks if we're lucky—then another fight over something—what?—not possible to know or predict, and certainly not to prevent . . . and then all this to go through again; and beyond that still another fight looming in the mist ahead, coming closer . . . and so on without end." But even while thinking these things he still would try to work through the current trouble because, as he would say, "There isn't anything else." And sometimes there occurred to him, uneasily, beyond all this gloomy reflection, an even more sinister thought: that their fights were not only unavoidable but also, perhaps necessary; for their passages of greatest tenderness followed hard upon their times of greatest bitterness, as if love could be renewed only by gusts of destruction.

Needless to say this point of view that marriages at their

best require profound conflict commands an entirely different notion of marriage counseling than the "Now, now, let's see if you can stop all this anger" school of well-intentioned traditional marriage treatment.

As we previewed earlier, psychologist George Bach has designed marital group therapy experiences specifically for teaching couples how to fight with each other vividly. Dr. Bach has suggested we consider husbands and wives as "intimate enemies"!

In a most important book under the title, *The Intimate Enemy*, Bach teaches principles of fair fighting, and how to spot, and counter, unfair fighting techniques.

To our mind, Bach tends toward another kind of evasion when he begins to emphasize the *immediate* fighting to such an extent that he proposes not to care anymore about the whole personal background story of either or both spouses; in fact, he insists such personal psychology is irrelevant; and he also seems to imply that what each person feels in the intimacy of inner feelings, and, yes, in the good old-fashioned unconscious, doesn't matter any more; all that counts is plenty of open fighting that is fairly conducted.

In the next section of this book, we will be emphasizing techniques of inner, attitudinal postures for each combatant spouse, that is, much more about each spouse's way of seeing himself and the meaning of life for him even as he sallies forth to marital battle.

However, the point here that should be entirely clear is that Bach's naturalistic concept of fighting in marriage, and his concepts for teaching people how to fight in marriage are indeed trailblazing door openers to a much more real and effective view of the marriage relationship.

It is reassuring also to find in a thoughtful religious counselor an awareness of the importance of teaching couples, in the words of Ecclesiastes, both "a time to love, and a time to hate..."

Gibson Winter of the Divinity School of the University of Chicago, an Episcopal minister, observes that "most famine today need more honest conflict and less suppression of reel ing." For those who would hide behind a simple-minded notion of a couple loving each other as one would love his God, Dr. Winter observes,

> We cannot find personal intimacy without conflict. Intimacy and conflict are inseparable in human life. This is true in the relationship between God and man. It is true in human relationships. . . . We become aware of the effort required to maintain an intimate relationship. We begin to see that our own personal lives can only grow as we make these efforts and live with others who accept and forgive us. The crisis of intimacy sometimes looks like the end of the marriage. When we are faithful to the covenant, this crisis becomes the beginning of the marriage.

Since this notion of the inevitability of profound difficulty in marriage is reasonably new, we should consider ourselves only at a beginning point of being able to instruct our marriage counselors and psychotherapists how to teach people to fight constructively in marriage.

And although we will shortly go on to suggest beginning principles for the marriage counselor to draw on in teaching couples *how to experience* their marital strains more productively, these principles to be added to other contributions such as Bach's teachings of *how to fight*, the important point is not the fun ('tis that) of the suggested concrete strategies, but rather the acknowledgment that marriage is a hell of a natural-crisis process. In general, we would suggest that the *how* of marital fighting and loving will yet be worked out through the efforts of many family researchers. The critical point of the hour, we have felt, is the need for a theory of marriage that acknowledges once and for all that marital fighting is inevitable, necessary, and desirable—not simply an unhappy byproduct of emotional immaturity or disturbance. The latter make for ineffective and immature fighting, or for a suppression of fighting with all their marriage-shattering consequences, but not for the fighting *per se* that is the legacy of all of us Adams and Eves.

CHAPTER NINE

CONCLUSION:

FAMILY LIFE AS A CRISIS CO-OP

FOR BECOMING

SELF-REGARDING PEOPLE

All of which dictates an entirely different concept of family life from our traditional Western picture of the family as a

haven,
fortress,
island of security,
oasis,
refuge,
warm hearth,
tender bosom.

Rather, we suggest that we consider the family a cooperative for emotional development (over and above its well understood roles vis-a-vis reproduction, economic provision, etc.) which supports each member's psychological needs to grow more secure in his image and belief in himself out of his being afforded a series of provocative, stressful, upsetting experiences with those who truly love him and whom he truly loves!

In an overview of the dramatically changing role of the family, psychiatrist Richard Cohen has pointed out how "the family represents the last bastion in which human emotion and experience is highly valued. Only in the family can a child experience the spontaneity, informality and infinite shades of variation of feeling and nuances of verbal and non-verbal communication."

Awareness of the inevitable, universal nature of injustice and betrayal in family life challenges us, as each such crisis in itself challenges us, to a redefinition of family life.

The goal of family life is to foster and enjoy growth through vaccinations of pain. However, let it be entirely clear that we are not suggesting that all family injustice and betrayal is healthy, desirable, or bearable. There are indeed life-and-death differences between therapeutic dosages for vaccinations and actually getting smallpox.

The family is a training lab for life-stress where training takes place under the watchful eye of those who care most, not strangers at all; indeed the trainers are equally vulnerable to their trainees' insults and jibes and injustices!

Granted, this business of training with people who really are involved with you has its serious limitations; and all too often we need the more objective and less involved outside professional helping person to help bind wounds and teach us more of how to grow through pain.

But the point of these observations is that much of the hell might be reduced if and when we learn to see our family hell as part of a process of potential growth.

This should not be so shocking an idea to most of us who already have come to accept that an awful lot of the helping of the psychoanalytic psychotherapist does indeed involve a hell of a process of deprivation and frustration and increasing rage and fantastic projection, all of which has as its intended culmination release to feel oneself in a freer way without being bound by introjected attitudes of another's earlier hatred (that was previously incorporated into the self identity).

Might we someday learn to teach children, and all of us, that family life is inextricably a world of conflict; and that successful family living means a never-ending sequence of learning through a struggle, not at all unlike Zeno's paradox, where one never reaches the end, until indeed there comes that end that marks the destiny of every family, and of every individual being.

But until then, since die we must, why not have some fun in the struggle? Even when we get "shafted," as we all do—bar none, not even the well analyzed, and the good analyzers.

For those of us who are the shoemakers of family life, that is, therapists, and other students of family life, there is some further fun in all our varied opportunities to study these unbelievably complex processes about which we know so little.

Elie Wiesel, perhaps the most awesomely penetrating commentator on the Nazi holocaust he survived, writes tragically-beautifully that the holocaust will henceforth forever press at man's very conception of his humanity. We would now add: man's very conception of his family life.

With Wiesel, we conclude this first half of our book that is our effort at contributing to a more honest theory of man's family-life troubles:

> To me, the whole event remains a question mark. I still don't know how man could have chosen cruelty. I still don't know how God could have allowed him such a choice. I still don't know why Jews kept silent. In fact, I know nothing.

Book Two

a book of "psychotechnology"—
or a manual of suggestions
for everyday marital coping

WORKING PRINCIPLES FOR SURVIVAL IN THE MARITAL INFERNO

In the chapters that follow, we present a variety of suggestions for how one might channel, pace, and otherwise call on his feelings for the hard, everyday business of marital hating, amidst, we trust, and in the interests of, much loving.

We will not be devoting ourselves so much to the overt what to dos *with the spouse so much as to the inner feelings one might cultivate for the lively, hard, but intriguing, and ever-challenging process of being one's own person while engaged in the always strangely perplexing and discomforting marital process.*

Less is said of the what to dos *for a variety of reasons. There is the already-excellent work of George Bach on training in actual martial [sic] techniques.*

Moreover, it is very much more this writer's natural interest to follow the inner experiencing of man in his marital processes rather than the He said *and* She said.

Ultimately, there is our conviction that one might do all the right things; and, yet, it will be inevitable in the intimacy of marriage, as in all human experience, that there will be deep pain and conflict as an organic natural part of the human process. And that much of joy of life is precisely in learning through the living out of the process—rather than having a happy marriage.

The suggestions that follow grow out of a background of real human experience; the author's and others' oh-so-many tears, other human fluids (sweat and blood, for example), and also laughs from deep down in the belly of our absurdities. It is likely these suggestions will be of some interest to other people ...

Any man who has no wife is not a man [i.e., a complete human being], for it is written: "Male and female He created them, and blessed them, and He called *their* name man" (Genesis 5.2).
—*The Talmud:* Yevamot 63a

R. Alexandri said: The world is darkened for him whose wife has died in his days [i.e., predeceased him], as it is written, "The light shall be dark because of his tent and his lamp over him shall be put out" (Job 18.6).

Rabbah b. Bar Hannah said in R. Johanan's name: To effect a union between man and woman is as difficult as the dividing of the Red Sea, as it is written: "God maketh the solitary dwell in houses; He bringeth out the prisoners unto prosperity" (Psalms 68.7). But is it really so? Did not Rab Judah say in Rab's name: Forty days before the embryo is formed, a heavenly voice goes forth and says: The daughter of so and so for so and so?—There is no difficulty: this applies to the first marriage, the earlier statement, to the second.

Rab Judah taught his son R. Isaac: Only with one's first wife does one find pleasure, as it is said: "Let thy fountain be blessed and have joy of the wife of thy youth" (Proverbs 5.18). Of what kind of woman do you speak? he asked him.—Of such as your mother, was the reply. But is this true? Had not Rab Judah taught his son, R. Isaac, the verse: "And I find more bitter than death the woman whose heart is snares and nets" (Ecclesiastes 7.26) and the son asked him: What kind of woman? He answered, Such as your mother?—True, she was a quick tempered woman but nevertheless easily appeased with a word.

R. Samuel b Unya said in the name of Rab: A woman [before marriage] is a shapeless lump [i.e., of undetermined character] and concludes a covenant only with him who transforms her into a useful vessel, as it is written: "For thy maker is thy husband; the Lord of Hosts is his name" (Isaiah 54.5).
—*The Talmud:* Sanhedrin 22a-b

—Above Talmud selections from Philip Goodman & Hanna Goodman. *The Jewish Marriage Anthology*. Philadelphia: Jewish Publication Society, 1965, pp. 25, 31–32.

And she put her arms round him under his shirt, but she was afraid,

afraid of his thin, smooth, naked body, that seemed so powerful, afraid of the violent muscles. She shrank, afraid.

And when he said, with a sort of little sigh: "Eh, tha'rt nice!" something in her quivered, and something in her spirit stiffened from the terribly physical intimacy, and from the peculiar haste of his possession. . . .

Yet, as he was drawing away, to rise silently and leave her, she clung to him in terror.

"Don't! Don't go! Don't leave me! Don't be cross with me! Hold me! Hold me fast!" she whispered in blind frenzy not even knowing what she said, and clinging to him with uncanny force. It was from herself she wanted to be saved, from her own inward anger and resistance. Yet how powerful was that inward resistance that possessed her!

He took her in his arms again and drew her to him, and suddenly she became small in his arms, small and nestling. It was gone, the resistance was gone, and she began to melt in a marvelous peace. And as she melted small and wonderful in his arms, she became infinitely desirable to him, all his blood-vessels seemed to scald with intense yet tender desire, for her, for her softness, for the penetrating beauty of her in his arms, passing into his blood. . . . She yielded with a quiver that was like death, she went all open to him. And oh, if he were not tender to her now, how cruel, for she was all open to him and helpless!

She quivered again at the potent inexorable entry inside her, so strange and terrible. It might come with the thrust of a sword in her softly-opened body, and that would be death. She clung in a sudden anguish of terror. But it came with a strange slow thrust of peace, the dark thrust of peace and a ponderous, primordial tenderness, such as made the world in the beginning. And her terror subsided in her breast, her breast dared to be gone in peace, she held nothing. She dared to let go everything, all herself, and be gone in the flood.

—D. H. LAWRENCE. *Lady Chatterley's Lover*. New York: Grove Press, pp. 226, 228–229. Text from the third manuscript version first published by Giuseppe Orioli, Florence, 1928.

In the Twisted World, as in any other, you are apt to discover yourself. But only in the Twisted World is that meeting usually fatal.

Familiarity breeds shock—in the Twisted World.

The Twisted World may conveniently (but incorrectly) be

thought of as a reversed world of Maya, of illusion. You may find that the shapes around you are real, while You, the examining consciousness, are illusion. Such a discovery is enlightening, albeit mortifying.

A wise man once asked, "What would happen if I could enter the Twisted World without preconceptions?" A final answer to his question is impossible; but we would hazard that he would have some preconceptions by the time he came out. Lack of opinion is not armor.

Some men feel that the height of intelligence is the discovery that all things may be reversed, and thereby become their opposites. Many clever games can be played with this proposition, but we do not advocate its use in the Twisted World. There all doctrines are equally arbitrary, including the doctrine of the arbitrariness of doctrines.

Do not expect to outwit the Twisted World. It is bigger, smaller, longer and shorter than you; it does not prove; it is.

Something that *is* never has to prove anything. All proofs are attempts at becoming. A proof is true only to itself, and it implies nothing except the existence of proofs which prove nothing.

—ROBERT SHECKLEY. *Mindswap.* New York: Delacorte, 1966, pp. 199–200 (*a novel of science fiction*)

CHAPTER TEN

TO BE A HUMAN BEING

IN ONE'S QUITE NATURAL ANGER

It is natural and right to feel anger.

Oh, *how* natural! Every day! And many moments through the day!

No, that doesn't at all mean that you have to be steaming and red-faced or red-gutted with anger inside of you all the time.

Yes, our more righteous readers, you are quite right that them's no way to live at all.

But the fact is that if we learn to trust the naturalness of our frequent, yes—everyday—experiences of anger, these emotions become quiet, blended themes in the overall symphony of our emotions and being.

We do urinate several times a day, don't we? And at any given point, we are building up the supply in the reservoir. Neither the period of buildup, nor the time when one actually needs to urinate generally represents that much of a noteworthy red-uretered crisis, does it? It becomes part of a natural, continuous cycle.

The analogy is not intended to be a literal one, although students of the language of feelings and unconscious symbolism will not miss the fact that there are all sorts of expressions about *holding your piss* as ways of saying that a person should hold on to his anger and not have to spray it, immediately, all over the place when he first gets to feel mad.

How can we say it most simply and with greater dignity?

The capacity to feel anger is a simple, natural part of our being for dealing with the complexity of life.

There are many things that anger us, and anger in itself is not necessarily anything more than a signal for our feeling that our best interests are being thwarted, or attacked, or about to be attacked; the anger is a signal to our then mobilizing various creative responses on our own behalf. Anger is a key dynamism in our thermostatic system for gauging our position in life at any given time.

Anger certainly finds its mark most of all at our intimates —our loved ones: Mothers! Fathers! Spouses! Children! Pets too!

Ah, but the trick is to know how to enjoy using the anger naturally!

Much of our anger operates unconsciously, that is, without our necessarily knowing or needing to know about it a lot of the time; as an inner signal in the rich stream of our constant unconscious computation of where we stand in the world and whether we should now be taking some kind of action to protect our interests.

There then follows a further level where an enormous amount of relief is available from enjoying picturing to oneself consciously the doing in of one's enemy; and since this is an inner picturing we're talking about, there need be no serious limit to the sadism and depravity and cruelty exercised in these modern-day voodoo rituals.

It is absolutely too unwieldy to go around all the time telling everybody how one is angry at them. There isn't enough time in the day. And, besides, the righteous ones are quite right that that is no way to live at all.

But what they don't know is that it's quite all right to do an awful lot of lopping off of your enemy *in your own mind*. As a matter of fact, this is the sine qua non of democracy. *They can't control your thoughts!* You can tell the President off without getting the FBI on to you—in fact, although this is a very frightening thought, you even can assassinate him for that horrible piece of legislation, because when you *think* about shooting him, you're not *really* doing him any harm at all; what you're doing is simply casting a mind movie to express that oft-repeated, perfectly natural expression, "I could shoot that man!"

Oh, oh, the righteous are upon us again: "Doesn't that kind of thinking lead to people shooting their Presidents?" they say aghast.

Without belaboring the point, the answer from virtually all data in psychology is *No*. In fact, the more comfortable one is about one's *feelings* of anger, the less likely one ever is to engage in terrible overt *acts*. Much more about this fundamental principle later.

Right now, let us consider even more deeply the enormous rewards available from this business of thinking-feeling-imagining your enemy getting clobbered by you.

Consider the many situations in this world where one normally feels absolutely overwhelmed and intimidated by the superior strength or power status of the other; rather than standing with downcast eyes, a broken heart, a feeling of being enslaved, how delicious to at least enjoy being able to stand next to that Boss or Landlord or Visiting Dignitary from the Big Plant or the Government-Funding Agency and think to oneself, "You son-of-a-bitch, I can see you coming in for a loan for a car someday when I'm the banker!" Or "I can see you running out in your underwear at night after I set your house on fire." And so forth, imaginative readers.

In fact, and mark this well, oh gentle reader who wishes to enlarge the sphere of his power on this troubled earth, there is a way of using such imagery not only for one's own inner release, but actually to accomplish otherwise quite unattainable interpersonal goals.

The secret is this: In those tough situations, like the Governor's reception, or the meeting with the Big One, or the visit of your parent to your home when you don't really want—or don't think it really right—to have all sorts of anger out in the open,

> *Think-imagine your anger in your best imagery production, all the while looking your enemy in the eye, and with a twinkle-sparkle of joy shining in your own eyes at your secret pleasures!*

You will be amazed and delighted to find that many things may happen that otherwise would never have come your way. The Terrible Big Boss may well turn to you with a sudden glimmer of respectful recognition and say something complimentary, and maybe right on the spot go on to set up further contact with you or reward for you that really was not in the wind till then. And that parent who had been talking down to you for yea these forty odd years may well look up with a kind of strangely respectful acknowledgment of you as a grown person.

How does this whole bit work? What's the *m-a-g-i-c*?

First of all, there is this delicious light of strength that comes into one's eyes when one is thinking of doing in one's enemy, and is enjoying his simple inward triumph, that communicates a sense of vigor; we carry our shoulders more erectly, our head stands more proudly on our shoulders, there is a tonic quality to our skin, in short, we look handsome and beautiful with a sense of liveliness and trust in ourselves. This attracts attention and respect!

Besides, there may well be some kind of ESP-type of communication at such moments, if not in the sense of some kind of actual thought-wave transmission that science has yet to lay its proving hands on (although there is surprising support for some kind of nonverbal communication between people), then at least on the basis of a kind of thinking on the part of the Other seeing the glow of life-joy in our eyes, particularly as we are focusing on them; the message they get from the universal language of such eyeball gestures is that of our sense of triumph and release from bondage, and then it isn't that hard for them to figure out, from within their own unconscious capacity to do the very same damn thing, that we have got them pinned up against the wall in our inner heart-minds.

And it's an old story that people stand up and take notice when you deal with them forcefully, especially when also fairly.

There is much to be gained in marriage from learning how to fight with one another openly; saying what we feel, but not promiscuously; sharing our angers with each other, but not overwhelming one another.

We now approach the many, many times when it really is essential, let alone desirable, actually to say something about our angry feelings to our spouse—just as in relationships with many other intimates where many of the same principles apply. But like good doctors, we certainly need to become masters of dosage, so that the good medicine helps us rather than kills us, let alone that we don't use too small, ineffectual dosages of something that might have helped us had we used it properly (we are also tempted to the analogy that too small doses may encourage the growth of further disease organisms rather than heal us).

If there is anything truly dramatic in the contribution of the new family-therapy procedures that came into the world of mental health in the last decade, it is that telling one's inti-

mate *like it is* can release people from the most horrible bond-
ages where they had turned their feelings against their own
selves.

We now have documentation after documentation of truly
dramatic instances where people who have been suffering
long-term, severe mental illnesses have been able to snap out
of the tragedy of their withdrawal, once gathered with their
family in a family interview which is conducted so as to really
hear the blocked-out messages of the *sick* one to his family—
the terrible anger that is in the withdrawal or strangeness. Lo
and behold, at least temporarily, the sick one may become suddenly alert, suddenly alive, suddenly encouraged, and the
seemingly normal ones, previously there to live out a phony
kind of sympathy for their poor family member trapped in his
strange thing of mental illness, have sometimes turned equally
rapidly into looking like really sick or psychiatrically symptomatic patients.

One story from the early days of the chance-discoveries of
family therapy is that of a veterans' hospital in which group
therapy was provided for the hospitalized mentally ill veterans, and another counseling group for their relatives. The
latter ran the usual gamut of giving the relatives a chance to
express their concern, anxiety, even anger at the sickness of
their relative, helping them to know how to talk to the patient,
and so forth, all the while playing out the distinction between
them poor sick ones, and us the healthy ones who are saddled
with learning how to be nice and fair to them. Somehow, it
developed that it might be a good idea to put the patients and
relatives together in a group; but what then happened is that
one staff member after another would come into this extended
patients and relatives group only to remark that they were
confused as to who the patients were and who the relatives
were! You couldn't tell the patients without a scorecard!

Again, we emphasize, the trick is to know how and when
and how much. Just how much anger one shares with the

other should be a function of the time, the place, and the situation. The greatest awareness of one's anger should be in oneself; it is generally wrong to tell one's spouse "everything" of one's anger. Say, for example, that a man in psychotherapy discovers his unconscious feeling that his wife is a so-called castrating woman. It would be folly for that man to go home to his wife that night and say: "You want to castrate me, you bitch!" However, the same man will indeed be putting his therapy learning to good work if he is able to recognize the next time he feels his wife belittling him and can speak up and say just that in everyday words: "You make me very angry by the way you speak to me."

Note that even in therapy, a situation where there is virtually unlimited freedom to experience one's anger, the freedom is less than the inner freedom in one's own mind. Thus, even for children who are invited to play their angers out more overtly in a play therapy experience, there are specific limits on how far the child may act out his anger even though he is given cap guns and hammers and whatnot with which to do *some* overt physical acting out. Adults in treatment are instructed that they may *feel* as angry as they wish, but they may not act out as the children do. Note too that for all parties in therapy, there are various technical devices introduced by the therapist to encourage and teach the patient to modulate his anger; for example, the level of anger should not be so intense that it cannot be turned off by the end of the session.

The more so is this true in family life. One does not have to express one's anger the minute one feels it—if at that moment a child needs attention. One should not have to express one's anger as totally vividly as one experiences it in one's own mind where pretty universally anger is experienced unconsciously as the equivalent of, or at least as approaching the boundaries of, wishing to kill another person; in our everyday talk we might keep these images on a more manageable level even though some of us who are more aware of our own minds may be able to realize that inside of ourselves we really are *feeling* like saying to our spouse, "Do drop dead—quite permanently!"

It is very much wrong actually to hurt another person in overt <u>acts</u> against the other's person, but to <u>feel</u> like hurting another is a natural expression of anger.

If there is any distinction that is vital to the survival of a marriage, and to the survival of the whole *goddamned* human race, it is just this one.

The plain, simple truth is that we all have to learn how to keep our cotton-pickin', destroyin' hands off of one another even when we feel—perhaps quite justly—like destroying one another. And the simplest reason for this principle is that if we don't, we're all going to end up destroyed to hell!

How glib are the rationalizations when people are in the heat of *their* red-faced hearts of anger!

"I don't care what happens to me!"

"He deserves everything he is getting, and better!"

Sure, and that's exactly how we all feel when, rightly or wrongly—generally quite naturally—we feel like the victims of another's miserable unfairness, or even his brutality.

Yet, it is sobering, sobering, sobering to remember how in virtually all husband-wife fighting—personally I've never seen an exception—both spouses *sincerely* feel themselves the victim, the aggrieved one, the beaten-on one!

The trick is to learn that there is an awful lot you can do with *emotional* techniques of anger that really provide a sense of release for one's anger.

The deeper trick is to learn that you *are* worth everything in the world, do deserve to stay alive, and therefore you, and all of us, should commit ourselves unambiguously to *the* fundamental rule we need for the survival of all of us, that is, we cut out *actual* destructiveness.

There is another terribly important reason why we must learn to commit ourselves not to hitting our spouse overtly, and that is that even in those situations where the hit in a sense really is not that physically hurting, and is even largely fair, so many of our spouses simply are unable to take it; with just a gesture of hitting, so many spouses see such a deep red—they feel such a fantastic sense of being fundamentally violated—that they are unable to bounce back to the relationship with us and keep it going. And, after all, the point of our anger most of the time is not to end the relationship, but to make it work better than it has been!

OK—now that we've laid down the truth of not overtly hurting the other, let's begin looking at the exceptions. We'd better! Human beings notoriously fail to live up to ideal principles—and if we want to help them-us, we had better know how to ride with many of their-our failings, even as we shoot for our ideal.

First, strangely enough, there is a tragically sizable group of spouses who ask to be abused; these are the people who solicit—for the most part, unconsciously—attacks against them by their spouses. And in a sense their spouses aren't as evil in their own right as it would look on the surface. Like that definition of a sadist: *The sadist is a person who is kind-hearted to a masochist!*

Tell these victims of marital scarring that they are asking to be victims, and you encounter the most stubborn kinds of denial imaginable. Their simplest defense of course is to hide behind the sheer illogic of it. "How can you possibly say that I want to be beaten?" "It's not that way at all. He's bigger than I. What can I do to stop him?"

Consciously, the victims really believe that there is nothing they can do. It takes enormous patience, and fairly complicated psychotherapeutic methods, to begin making a dent in this kind of a system.

One extremely attractive young woman who quite regularly suffered blows from her spouse began to allow a glimmer of awareness of the possibility that she was asking for it when we were able to think out together how there are women who feel trapped by passes and don't have any idea at all that there is a kind of cueing going on from their body gestures that invites men to come at them with sexual overtures. (Sometimes there is such cueing playing a distinct part even in inviting more dangerous kinds of assault or rape.) Our attractive-victim-of-the-marital-beating, entirely sure of herself in such situations, knew that she was icily and steely entirely able to turn off any possible sexual interest in her. I kept suggesting to her that a similar kind of conviction and gestural defense system is what worked for many other women who had brutish husbands; that in her case there was a kind of taunting and tantalizing on her part that enraged the bull of her husband to come after her; and then that she was able to experience the attack as somehow strangely comforting in its continuity of the disasters of her childhood, while at the same time using the attack for her own purposes as a way of saying, "No matter how much you (and life) attack me, none of you will ever break me, I'm invincible!"

To all victim readers, we have this to say: Study after study of marital affairs and other human interactions tells us that when a person puts out firmly and with dignity and assurance the message of their intent not to be hurt by another, most attacks will cease or diminish.

There is social psychological laboratory evidence, for example, that once the sadistic attacker has inflicted injury on his victim, he comes to view his victim as even lesser in value than before and then even more deserving of further injury than was the case before. This is a most fascinating cue indeed to the terrible sequences of destructiveness that take place between some couples . . . and in some larger situations of genocidal attacks against an entire victim-people.

Oh, (dear) victims! do (please) avail yourselves promptly

of professional help—if there is enough in you that would want to learn how not to be beaten; also, if you want to help your sadists—often they're relatives or friends, aren't they?—from hurting themselves by being bastards, for inside they too truly suffer a loss of decency that becomes irreparable after a time, or after they sortie into a degree of destructiveness of a truly inhuman degree.

Back now to more everyday instances of overt attack in marital warfare. Gentle reader, let us add now an exception to the rule in what for some will be a strange language of contradiction (but in truth 'tis the language of dialectics, or the fact that the very truth of a principle often has as its source some measure of experiencing its anti-truth, just as resistance to a disease often has as its origin some measure of exposure to the very toxins of that disease).

As every clinician knows, the truth is that overt marital fighting is far more common than most of our literature acknowledges, and even among quite decent people, and very much including those who are on their way to an ultimate kind of making it in their marriages. Just as common sense demands that we get to be more sensible about the way we handle certain truths about sexual infidelity once we have the Kinsey data to tell us that it happens and happens and happens, so too it is in our interest to come to some kind of realistic terms with the facts of overt attack in marital relationships—in order that we may pursue our own best interests.

The sequence in the oh-so-difficult business of marriage might go something like this: a couple first discovers that it is very much within the capacity of both of them, like all us human critters, to be damned destructive. Somewhere, fairly early in a marriage, there may be a button-tearing, face-slapping, arm-punching, or dish-throwing exchange. Since it is early in marriage, at a time all sorts of delicious sexual passions are on the surface, and with all the flexibility of youth, the couple doesn't quite have to go down dead on this occasion, and among other things can bounce back to the alternative passions of making love. However, more important, the incident, or a handful of such incidents, arms both spouses with a terrifying awareness that human beings really can be destructive as hell, and therefore that there had damn well better be some machinery for regulation of just how far everybody goes if they are going to survive this intimacy called marriage!

What happens then, optimally, is a kind of unconscious decision to avoid violence in the future so that one is not the trigger of a counter violence from the other. Also, the pain of these experiences leads the spouses unconsciously to begin searching for many alternative techniques for managing and expressing their anger.

Now, let us go on to follow this couple through a few years more. Of course, we are assuming that they are not stuck with any version of one of them playing the bully role of overt attacks against the other as a victim. We are also assuming that like virtually all of us—except for the really troubled ones who can't stand finding out they have any trouble— the marriage becomes somehow more complicated: bitternesses have deeper roots, there is a more permanent sense of sadness over the ideal that both now know will never be, there are periods of great demoralization, and peaks of pain, and wishes to get out—along with lots of good things, we trust, and so wish everybody. Somewhere in the course of this later complexity of it all, there often unfolds a renewed scene of a burst of overt aggression against a spouse's person.

So often, this episode has as its intent bringing the couple down to the wire—to an ultimate test of whether or not to stay together.

On the one hand, having pretty much assumed that both partners learned earlier just how dangerous violence could be, and had implicitly committed themselves to avoiding such risks, given now such an insufferable insult of renewed attack, there seems to be every justification in the world for the victim of this onslaught to depart.

And considering the terrible rage that burst into an attack, the attacking spouse apparently has every wish and sense of justification to be rid of his partner.

Yet, what deep meaning there can be if after such an attack there can follow a deep crisis of hurt and despair in which the attacker can yield to acknowledge his caring for the other and, yes, contriteness for his action, but along with a really self-respecting explanation of the depth and justification of the angry feeling that was and still is; and if the victim in turn can acknowledge, in all his hurt, the reciprocal of caring and wanting the stinkin' spouse attacker—along with a clear definition of future inviolability to physical attack, yet with understanding that there was indeed reason for the attacker's enormous anger that needs to be listened to as separate from the attack itself.

Let's say it very simply now. Overt hitting in a marriage is wrong. However, there will sometimes come exceptions, still quite wrong, but often it will be most human and wise to allow these as exceptions, and to develop from them a long-range commitment to the truth that overt attacking is wrong, as well as to learn the equally important truth that it is essential to build a machinery for honest expression of feeling if there is to be any kind of relationship.

Remember in another way too that <u>feelings</u> are not at all the same as <u>actions</u>: Our feelings of anger in no way <u>really</u> punish or hurt the other party in a literal sense.

It is astounding how many people become emotionally upset by the unconscious feeling that their angry feelings at another somehow will do actual harm to the other. There is much in normal childhood that intends to build natural devices for warding off the possible effects of one's angry dreams and wishes on one's loved ones—especially one's parents. The business of stepping over cracks in the street has been analyzed psychoanalytically to have something to do with the oft-repeated ditty, "Step on a crack—break your mother's back!" And children go into virtual panics after having dreams of the deaths of their parents, certainly dreams in which they go even further and play a direct part. Like pushing daddy onto the tracks in front of the train! Or just plain standing there fearing (the disguised form of wishing) that he may fall over in front of the train!

It is a recurring phenomenon among the severely mentally ill that the poor patient's personality is often one of great innocence. Such people have not learned to feel their anger is perfectly OK; and so when their anger builds in them, as it must in life—and even more so for innocents because they become so passive or helpless or vulnerable to injustice, and such vulnerability only necessitates greater anger inside them —they cannot stand themselves, and they fear themselves to be so evil that they sentence themselves to imprisonment in withdrawal and mental illness.

Many people are amazed in coming to a child therapist's office to find that standard equipment includes such things as guns—*play guns, of course*. But it is not by chance that some children aren't at all sure these are play guns, and occasionally the seemingly-normal parents of a psychotic child have to ask to make this distinction!

In my own office, the paradox is the more poignant because people soon discover from literature in the waiting room and my library and whatnot my deep commitment to various research and social action on behalf of the evolution of a more nonviolent man; and a fair number of people coming to consult me to begin with are Quakers or members of one or another peace-caring groups.

The point, of course, is that to *wish*, to *feel*, to *imagine* is not the same as to *do*, to *hurt*, or to *destroy* for real.

I have spent many a dramatic moment in psychotherapy, especially with the sicker or more psychotic children, watching human beings learn this principle. It is just fantastic to see the shakiness with which a disturbed child may pick up a play gun. It is just fantastic to see how terrified he is of pointing it at the other person. It is just fantastic to see how often he is prepared to turn it on himself rather than point it at the other party. I have seen and experienced the unbelievable depth of terror of such children crying out with all their hearts as if for real survival. And it is such fantastic relief for them to learn a natural playfulness with these toy weapons so that they too can experience the animal-human legacy of us all to be able to feel angry, to be able to wish our worst enemies dead, but to trust the fundamental distinction that wishing these people dead doesn't kill.

I would offer the startling speculation that all too often in the history of man decent people may have killed others almost as a relief for their feelings—to get away from feared feelings bursting within them of wishing to hurt another intimate:

> It is almost better to get it over with.
> To be a criminal.
> To be a destroyer.
> And then to laugh perhaps in seeming not-
> caring as one joins the genocidal pack
> running wild.
> Triumphing over all the existential dilemmas
> of life.
> Ha-ha, ha, we're bigger than life itself!
> Nothing can touch us!
> The terror is no longer! Neither of de-
> stroying! Nor of being destroyed!

**Too much anger eats away at our own insides;
for our own sakes, we should seek to control
our anger thermostatically, to use the good
stuff of our anger for natural self-defense,**

but to leave plenty of room for loving, and caring, and befriending, and quietness, and many other delicious passions in the symphony of our emotional life.

Ah, those of our more gentle readers whom we earlier twitted as the "righteous ones," and who have survived reading this far in the chapter, your deserved relief is here at last. You see, we really do agree that too much anger is trouble.

Lots of trouble!

Too much anger doesn't hurt the enemy; it burns us up. Too much anger is destructive of us. You can *blow* a gut. You can *bust* up your marriage. You can *explode* an artery.

It is characteristic of the good fighter that he knows how to pace himself.

On the other hand, too little anger doesn't keep the furnace of one's life and one's marriage warm enough to give off any heat. There is a range within which anger should be developed. Good marital fighting, and good inner anger regulation, is managed by thermostats of our own self-awareness and discipline.

It is also an everyday clinical phenomenon—this also relates to our earlier discussion of fears of becoming actual destroyers—that people who are too angry, even if they have mastered their fears of possibly becoming destroyers, become depressed, and feel cruddy, and crappy, and ineffective, and lonely, and depersonalized. Why? Because they are just too damned angry at all of life; which is always beautiful, even when it is lousy; which is lovable, even when it's hatable; which stars with miracles of nature, even as it involves horrible injustices, and the uncaring of our gods and nature.

To be turned on is to be a symphony of feelings, and not one feeling crowding out the others. It is really unnatural, and dangerous, to be too angry, or too often angry; and we don't need to belabor this truth.

CHAPTER ELEVEN

PREPARING

FOR JUST HOW

TERRIBLY BAD

IT GETS!

The surest way to drown if you get into trouble in the water is to thrash about desperately trying not to drown; while the way to maximize chances for survival is to yield to the fact that you are in trouble and to trust that you can count on a certain reserve of floatability if you let go to it.

No, the truth is that I am not at all sure that I could do this were I in bad trouble in the water. Although I know that I have gotten somewhat better at yielding to the water over the years as I've tried to improve my swimming in general— which also involves a kind of living out of how one deals with fears of being engulfed by the water. (There is an intriguing and apparently often deeply effective approach to psychotherapy called *hydropsychotherapy*, pioneered by Lily Wiener of California; she works with the patient in the water, focusing on all the resistances and uptightnesses against water—and against the threats of death that all of life involves, seeking to arrive at a posture of yielding and calm effectiveness for mastery of the environment on the part of the patient.)

It is also interesting to think of the several Oriental martial or fighting techniques that are based on the concept of absorbing the energy of the enemy's blows—going *with* the blows rather than against them—and thereby being able to mute the power of the attack.

113

Or in our own Western world of automobile accident-tragedies, it is intense rigidity of defense against the oncoming whip that often is at the bottom of one's injury; as many a stunt man knows, if you let yourself go with the fall, you can perhaps come up unscathed in situations that will break the more brittle bones of the rest of us fairly readily.

In psychotherapy of individuals, those who are fortunate enough to proceed through a deep sequence to a fairly significant climax of release of themselves to greater self-love and self-respect find that one of the exciting climaxes comes with a kind of living out of one's death. Often there is a dream of dying. And while under other circumstances such a dream would represent the ultimate terror of hell, and a prediction that the worst kind of future is being forged unconsciously for us, something about this dream at the point that it comes, and in the way in which it is experienced, says instead that one is now strong enough to face and brave the awareness that ultimately there is no survival; thereby to come out the more alive, the more vigorous for the living that lies ahead until the time comes when down we must go. Again here we see a kind of strength that comes from yielding to the not-strong part of ourselves.

And so it is in marriage distress. He and she who are prepared for how terrible it will be at times—how utterly painful, demoralizing, and devastating—may paradoxically find that somehow it isn't *quite* as demoralizing, painful, and devastating as it could have been.

It can almost get to be fun! For in all its sadness, it can almost be a fun challenge. Just like living can be fun even though one has come to terms with the fact that we really are going to die.

Husbands and wives are far better off when they learn that in the course of marital fighting a good deal of unfairness, exaggeration, and extremes is natural.

(For the philosophically knowledgeable, we say on with the dialectics.)

Previously, we referred to the notion that there are many ways of fighting fairly as opposed to fighting unfairly. And that good fight training is a wise idea for all of us. And, yet, from the point of view of our interest in the inner symphony that is in all of us, we now add that even successful graduates of fight-training courses had best be prepared for tests of unfairness and exaggerations and extremes; for it is precisely through these that one learns how to be fair rather than unfair, and it is these experiences that somehow provide the tonic for going on to get better and decent precisely because one has tasted some of the lousiness and indecency of it all.

There are many reasons for human beings becoming so unfair. For one thing, it is true as previously mentioned that in our inner feelings our anger inevitably is experienced unconsciously as akin to inner images of killing; so that when you get a message that your spouse wishes you done in, you ought to realize that the fact that he or she feels like this is not unique, nor is it inherently evil, and most likely it isn't *really* what the other wants or plans to do in actuality. Needless to say, the latter distinction is a particularly crucial one (for the naive: this last sentence is written tongue-in-cheek!).

Intriguingly enough, it need not concern most of us, especially those of us who know that feelings of anger are being experienced and expressed. We have data from George Bach, who conducted a brilliant study of *actual* spouse killers, which showed that such couples had been living in "fight phobia"—an inability to negotiate aggression in the open—and not at all with the excessive fighting one might naively imagine in marriages that end up in a real murder.

Previously, we also discussed how human beings are part of the whole tapestry of nature in which the truth is that unfairness and extremes are indeed natural phenomena of life; and apparently that's the way our human-being machinery is built at the fabricating plant too; let alone, as we pointed out earlier, that we learn from the storms of hell that nature unleashes on us to model ourselves after her.

But most of all, it seems to me, much of the unfairness in marital and other fighting is like the "120" on the accelerator gauge of our cars. We know that there is this huge potential range in our machinery, and it is somehow natural to do a certain amount of testing and proving to convince ourselves that we really could choose to drive 120 mph—in human affairs, we mean that we really could be that lousy if we wanted to. But please, my peers, stop me; and please, my own insides, stop me!

> So I'll try it out. Just a bit to find out what will happen. And if, God forbid, neither you nor I stop me, I may get so terrified that I really may not be able to stop. Like throwing good money after bad. Pretending *I don't care.* Because I'm in such trouble already, what the devil difference will it make!

Our minds operate much like computers searching through all the accumulated data for just what we want to say; in a good heated marital fight the machinery tries out many bits, including such part-truths or truths-of-the-moment as "I wish I had never married you." We should not believe that anything our rival spouse says is fully intended or the whole truth of his feelings, nor should we believe anything we think of is the full measure of what we feel and believe.

Another reason marital fighting is often wild is that there is much in our computer-like minds that operates not so much with pinpoint accuracy as to what we really feel or know, but like a computer searching through all its accumulated data file for just what it is we want to say. The result in a good heated fight is that the machinery zooms off to find all relevant ammunition. "Let's see now, here's a sentence," says the computer; "I'll try it." "You are a lousy, miserable jerk, and I wish I had never married you," screams a spouse—not so much because they really wish they had never married, but because in the search for weaponry for the fight it seems right to try out that bit from the storehouse of possible fighting sentences. Unfortunately, all too many of us in this culture have been taught to believe as true and fully-intended anything the other person says, and all too often the harsh, quite undesired result is that two people who really didn't want to break up with each other do.

Remember what we were trying to learn about how *feelings* are not the same as *actions*. Here is a variation on the same theme: *Feelings,* however true, are not necessarily the actual *plan for action.*

Or another way of saying it, one's *feeling* is not one's whole *person.*

Or another way of saying it, that however true is one's feeling in *part,* it is not the *whole* of a person's feelings.

Unhappily, any and all of these distortions abound in our culture where there is a hypocritical emphasis on the literalness of everything that is said, rather than our enjoying teaching all of us to tap our capacity to perceive the more true symbolisms and inner meanings of our feeling-messages to one another; so that people would learn not to pick up any one element and blow it out of proportion.

Especially when it comes to the dread business of divorce do many people in our culture become so frightened and overwhelmed that they do not know how to fight; and often surrender to the spouse's first mention of their wish to divorce as if 'twere already all over; and act as if it isn't really tearing them apart—rather than try to fight for the marriage, perhaps then still to lose, and now all the more painfully because one made it clear that he or she really wanted to hold the very spouse who is apparently wanting out.

Needless to say, the same obtains for the products of our own minds too. It is part of the huge network of fallacies by which we seem to live that most of us are taught also to believe that anything *we* think of must be the truth of what we really feel or believe; and so when our mind plays with wishing for divorce—partly because we feel like this, partly because we're trying to try it out for size in a fight—some people end up talking themselves into believing this is what they want, now, immediately—what's that lawyer's telephone number?

In a later chapter, we will be discussing more fully this terrifying matter of divorce. The larger point here is that we need to learn that the minds of all us human beings—yes, our spouses and yes, us—are capable of *any* thought; under varying circumstances, from stress, to alcohol, to LSD, to sleep deprivation, to psychoanalytic free association, to dreams, to artistic creativity, and on and on, our minds are able to range over a full galaxy of feelings of the most gorgeous sort and of the most heinous and destructive sorts; this is the genius of our mind; and human maturity involves being able to bear some consciousness of these thoughts while leaving it to quite mature and soulful searching just which of our mind's productions we will really honor and select to act on as our true foreign policy. It really is better that we are capable of reviewing a variety of alternatives in our own minds, isn't it? This way we really have a choice what to select as our actual operational policy in life and aren't stuck with the first thing that comes to mind.

So many people are so terrified of their feelings that they seek never to feel. This is a kind of psychological death seen all too often.

On the other hand, to feel too much, that is, to be unknowing how to yield to the flow of our various thought-feelings with a knowledge that it is within our capacity and responsibility to select just those we will really act on, can be agonizing; this is a kind of psychological flooding seen in some people who are running helter and skelter, with this or that piece of emotionalism always showing in a confusing cascade; these are people who may be quite charming, but in whom one senses a basic lack of simple stability of feeling cared for and a resulting inability to rest without great activity.

Either extreme of being unfeeling or of feeling too much is murder for marital relationships. There are millions of mates in America who are dying a slow death with the rage they feel at spouses who are in a turned-off state of being unavailable to feelings. In communities where there are many engineering companies, psychotherapists often speak of an "engineer's syndrome" to refer to people who have turned to *things* so as to be away from *feelings* (rather than because of the fun and meaningfulness of working with things). It is not a syndrome all engineers suffer, nor is it exclusive to that profession. It is found on every level of life in all those people who run from their potential emotional richness.

So how do you do it? How do you go about feeling an awful lot, and yet not getting sucked up into being overly emotional and reactive to everything? In different cultures man has evolved a variety of ideas for trying to get at something of an optimal state of emotional aliveness or tone without being sucked up into being a super-bubbling exploding atom pile.

In our Western world of psychoanalysis, we have developed some firm notions about a part of the personality that we call the *self-observing ego*. This is a part of us, as it were, that goes about looking on what we are otherwise feeling in our various relationships and experiences; and which, in effect, lets us know, like a director off-stage, that even as we are acting our role in a play, the *part* that we feel at any given point is not *all* of us. Thus, this fellow, the self-observing ego, does a bang-up job in psychotherapy where he is the one who realizes that Truth (with a capital T) is not in the immediate moment of every free association, but rather in the central themes that will somehow emerge from certain special moments and mainly from many repeated moments of free association, and even more than that, in the thrust of certain kinds of implications for self-correction and advancement of ourselves that will come out of listening to many hours of data from within ourselves. So that at any given moment of experiencing, for example, in feeling a towering, destructive rage toward another human being, truth is not wholly or necessarily in that experience, even though it is true we are feeling genuinely in the here and now. Indeed, if one goes on to flood with never-ending anger toward yon person, even as any given moment of this anger is genuine and authentic, to our still deeper genuineness of self-observation, the larger implication of too many moments of such anger will be that it is in our own interest to learn to quiet down the anger, and to seek a more constructive basis for relating to our fellow human beings so that we do not burn our own selves up.

In entirely different language, in fact in language that sounds contradictory of the above, there is a fairly similar approach to disciplined use of one's emotions in the Zen attitude of *not being too conscious of one's self*. It is strange how this very phrase would seem to imply the opposite of the observing of one's self that is the job of our Western self-observing ego. And yet, like other dialectics, we have seen any number of times where opposites somehow can be intrinsically similar.

The Zen posture intends that we learn not to be conscious of the *immediate effort* to shoot an arrow from our bow, or to drive our car, or to joust with our spouse in battle, but to let things, like marital fighting, happen as they must, leaving ourselves aware that there is so much more of our inner selves that exists, and deserves to be savored, than should be tied up in a too-intense concentration on shooting a bow, or shooting a spouse!

It is a way of relieving one's self of the self-consciousness that makes many a baseball batter clutch up. And, yet, by freeing himself from too intense self-observation, by allowing himself to be natural, the batter with un-self-conscious swing will see the ball coming precisely out of not getting that uptight about the immediate moment or effort to see the ball. So just as we learned from the Western self-observing ego, what we are feeling or doing is not all of us at all. And we can go about doing what we're doing while leaving a lot of us free to experience at another level.

It is bad enough that often we must feel blue when fighting times must be lived out. It is wise not to add to this blueness by feeling angry at our spouse "because you are making me feel lousy." It is tough enough to be upset without being upset about being upset!

It is just as Franklin Roosevelt said, "The only thing you have to fear is fear itself!"

Even when the degree of problems in a marriage has reached proportions that do indeed represent a mental health problem—it really is hurting and it really is serious—it is still wisest to recognize how underlying universal dilemmas are nonetheless involved at the base of our particular hell. It is good to remember that much marital problems, and much of all problems, are a universal aspect of humanness.

This being the case, even when by every standard of our natural feeling our spouse is a miserable rat for giving us such a hard time, it behooves us to remember that our spouse is not a rat for being a rat!

It certainly is critical to remember that we are not rats whenever someone else makes us feel like a rat. Remember our earlier discussion of the work of Albert Ellis and his associates in rational-emotive psychotherapy. Ultimately, the only person capable of making one feel lousy is one's self. It is only if we agree in our own minds that we are rats that we are going to feel lousy when somebody else calls us that. Otherwise, we say to ourselves something like this, "I am being called a rat, but damned if I am; I feel angry over being called a rat, and I will be damned if I am going to feel that ratty about myself when I am not."

Why is our spouse-enemy doing all this to us?

Usually because spouses have to do their thing—not because it's *us*.

Spouses usually are not malicious because they are out to wipe *us* off the face of the earth. For the most part, our spouse's anger springs from the anxiety that is inevitable in all human beings as we all are forced to search for the strength with which to live our troubled lives. In that sense, we should seek to reconcile ourselves to some outbursts of our partners as inevitable, and so too to our own, as we both express our humanness and limitations.

The largest limitation of all is that we are all mortals; and this scares an awful lot of us people in more ways than we generally allow ourselves to recognize. We are all beautifully full of potential, but oh, so full of so many, many weaknesses. Certainly for a long time to come, man's evolution challenges us to a largely uncharted, difficult task of experimenting with the many-sided beautiful-terrible qualities of our being. Just that job is enough to make us all scared enough, to make us all cranky enough, to make us all crappy enough, to give each other a perpetually hard time. So sweat it, and fight it, man, but don't take it so personal-like. We're all in the same boat!

And for God's sake, stop worrying about how you look to the neighbors!

Of all the wasteful, unproductive bits that tie people's energies up, and virtually insure that they will make ten thousand more mistakes than they otherwise might, the worst is the one of shaping one's behavior not for and from our own insides, but with an eye to the galleries—the audience.

Granted, it is understandable that we would like to make a good show; and it is perfectly reasonable that *some* of our behavior in this world be aimed at doing just that.

But, over and over again it has been demonstrated that too much of an emphasis on showing ourselves to others, rather than showing ourselves to ourselves, is doomed to lead us into every variation of neurosis known to the macabre mind of the devil of nature. (This too is an area of emphasis by the rational-emotive therapist about which we wrote some earlier.)

As related to marital fighting in particular, be assured that there is no such thing as showing off your perfect marriage in this world! For everyone of us knows the real score that there ain't no such thing at all for all that many of us consciously live out the cultural hypocrisy and idiocy of making believe that there are good marriages without any serious problems. So that everyone of us knows unconsciously that those who show off their all-perfect marriage are the biggest liars of all, whether consciously or unconsciously.

"How are you?" is a standard everyday query from one person to another that is so often hollow and false. So often a sallow-faced, sad-eyed second person nods compulsively and says, "Fine, fine, thank you." It's downright funny to see how when sometimes people answer honestly that they are not in very good shape, the questioner is likely enough to give them a quick brush-off, not wanting to hear. But it really is even greater fun for the sad-sallow one to hold to his daringly honest answer, and to insist on it; in fact, often he will be a bit less sad for just such moments.

By the same token, how good it can be to say boldly, and even with a twinkle of humor not only, "Lousy today," but, sometimes, if it seems right in that relationship, to add, "Joan and I had a stinkin' fight; boy, marriage is sure a full-time job, isn't it?" More often than not, a vigorous kind of truth like this will win a friend in the questioner who was otherwise hurrying on his own selfish way through a formality that didn't mean a darn thing.

CHAPTER TWELVE

ENJOYING

THE TROUBLE OF IT ALL

Yes, *enjoying* it all—to a degree, anyway. Let's face it. All of life—including our ubiquitous marriage problems—really is painful. And there is an awful lot of sadness and fear.

In fact, at many moments, if one does not experience a fair measure of pain and fear, one's troubles get worse!; because our recognition of our vulnerability, and our yielding to it, is part of the wellspring of strength from which we bounce back!

Still psychology has discovered in the world of emotions that it is not necessary, indeed, it is not natural, to be simply one emotion at a time; if we listen to the small sounds within us, even as we are crying our hearts out, often we will hear a counterpoint of a kind of relief and pleasure in being able to feel sorry for ourselves; and if we look at the tears streaming down the happy faces of so many people, say at a wedding, we have a persuasive reminder that 'tis more than "tears of happiness" that shine forth from those eyes.

So, even as we suffer pains of marital conflict and hurt, it is possible to sit back and enjoy it, even "to get into it" and enjoy it with a kind of wry mirth, sometimes even a kind of roaring laughter at one's self, certainly at our antagonist, and even at the whole impossible institution of marriage.

The following principles are applications of such acceptance of the two-sidedness of our situation; following them may in turn help lay a groundwork for the kind of pleasure and sense of humor about which we are talking.

We would be wise to feel grateful for the stimulation of confrontations and challenges by our spouse.

Such clashes challenge us to grow in the areas of our greatest personal weaknesses—both in regard to qualities which are lacking in us, as well as to tone down exaggerated aspects of ourselves at which our partner, wisely, is shooting away.

Also, the very moments of our deepest despair often precede or lay the groundwork for a possibly immense deepening of our creative strength and joy. After awhile, one gets to recognize this rhythm; and then even when one hits black moments of hell, one can anticipate a kind of welling-up of a deeper resolve to live, and to create, that can follow the very experience of feeling we are up against it and virtually running out of our last strengths. How sad it is for those people who in their childhood are too indulged and spared too much tension, so that when they face challenges of life in later years, they tend to despair too quickly and do not trust themselves to sink to a depth of pain as a way of preparing a thrust of growth. Needless to say, how tragic too is the fate of those who are so crushed by evil in their growing experiences that they do not have inner reservoirs into which to dip. Both the terrible and the seemingly too-good childhood destroy people. Many suicides represent a statement of a black terror that no deeper reserve is waiting inside, and so people cannot bear to go on living out the process of surrendering to their agonies because they cannot believe they could ever bounce back. Yet, for many of the rest of us, the terror of being terrified can be far lessened if we but learn to trust the beauty of our regenerative capacity.

So it is in so many areas of human experience. "You don't appreciate what you have until you are sick." A deep and seemingly insurmountable anguish is considered a necessary precursor of *satori*-peacefulness in Zen. A heightening of powerful anxiety often precedes truly dramatic growth in psychoanalysis. It is living through our human difficulties that often sharpens the edge of our awareness of life's beauty, the gift of health, the challenges of growth, and so on.

Even when we hate, we may love!

It is not true that we only love *or* hate the other. At most moments, our feelings are a combination of the two; and even at the most intense moments of either passion, the other is still deeply represented within us. We have already referred to the truth that in sexual union there is a deeply subtle role to the aggressive and angry and hating emotions orchestrating symphonically with the overriding passions of desire and affection for the other and love; it is the absence of such symphonic complementarity that marks many symptoms of sexual malfunctioning—and especially, a real absence of pleasure.

In marital fighting, even the moments filled with our bitterest hate do and may carry at one and the same time our love. How good it is to know this before one might act too strongly, only to realize too late the damage done a person and a relationship one loves very much.

An excellent emotional exercise in the heat of marital battle is to conjure up (silently! for Macy's doesn't really tell Gimbel's!) just how much one cares for one's now quite-hated spouse; so as to experience one's hate and love as coexisting streams of feeling.

CHAPTER THIRTEEN

THE KILLER ISSUES

I. SEX AT HOME

AND AWAY FROM HOME

Sex is fun and healthy too. Have lots of it in as mutual an arrangement for pleasure as can be! Often (but not always), this can even mean times when you don't like each other that much!

Whoops, the righteous ones will now blow their cools again!

How can you ask of me to have sex with (him) (her) when I can't stand (him) (her)?

I'm no whore!

OK, righteous ones, get off my back; let's make it really clear that there are certainly times when there is a kind of bitterness between spouses, and a kind of despair, and disrespect, and a need to be apart that precludes sexual relations; and to sex at those times is indeed to whore immorally with one's emotions.

But there are lots of other times in the never-ending seasonal changes of marital relationships where in a way there's a kind of *fooey-on-you* attitude between the spouses, but not one that is hot with rage or that much bitterness; and it is more a state of you're-a-pain-in-the-neck and half-jerk too, just like we all are, a kind of deromanticizing of the relationship that is a recurring part of the natural sequence of our

129

human affairs, and there really are a whole bunch of good reasons for having sex at such times.

Probably the best reason is that if you want to break out of the rut of this kind of lack of interest in one another, and in life, try sex! It's one of the finest cocktails around.

Another good argument is that just as one comes to a stage in marriage where one decides to stay because it is—well —practical (although you'd love that absolutely enticingly fresh new critter down the block), and you in effect now agree that it's mutually advantageous to go on having meals together, and bringing up the kids, and continuing as an economic unit, why, it's just plain good pragmatic sense also to get what you can sexually with each other!

Whoops, the righteous ones have just split another gut.

"*Get what you can!*" That's just what you sound like, you have no morals, you're just out for anything you can get! Well, I value my body too much to treat it in that way.

We disagree thoroughly. Righteous ones, we think you don't value your body at all enough to see to it that you give your body, that is, yourself, enough of the natural pleasures of life; and just because there is some anger over problems with your spouse getting in the way doesn't mean that you should give up entirely a life pleasure that is that important. You don't stop eating most of the times when you have those vicious fights, do you?

Another "funny thing" happens when sex is treated as something for one's self; an awful lot of the hangups that may spoil sexuality for both sexes now tend to fade out. In clinical practice, we find that many of the psychosexual problems men and women experience derive from their feeling that they are performing, or obligated to perform, *for their spouse,* rather than *for themselves.*

Having to do something for someone else is intrinsically infuriating. And being too much infuriated, especially coupled with not knowing how to be out for one's self, is likely to get you hung up. But if you're out for yourself (gosh, doesn't that sound selfish?), then you really try to make things work, because it's fun. It's like capitalism. (Oh, that doesn't sound quite as selfish now, does it?) It's making a living for yourself.

A patient in psychotherapy dreamt that his father-in-law went bankrupt, and that his mother-in-law turned on her husband in great anger for his having failed *her.* The poor man was so upset that for a moment he teetered on the brink of having a heart attack; but then he rallied into a huge rage at the realization of his wife's unbelievable unfairness in complaining of her loss without having the slightest notion of how much of a loss he, husband, was living through for himself!

So let us offer a redefinition—one that will also stand us in good stead later when we get to the business of separateness.

Selfishness, the popular word for an undesirable character trait, we will say, is when you're out for yourself *at the expense of another.*

On the other hand, *self-love* is when you're out for yourself as the primary person in this world that you intend to please, and *should!*

And it's an old story, now documented by infinite research, that when you get to like yourself, and you are producing for yourself, it's then really fun to extend lots of yourself also to others, as a kind of joy about living that comes naturally.

Couples that get together in reasonably satisfying arrangements for their sexuality have fun! There will be times when one spouse will want sex more than the other, but often the second spouse will be able to be a reasonably willing partner knowing that it all comes out even in the long run, and knowing that their participating is not coerced or phony because times when it really is wrong to have sex with the enemy will be declined.

Because such couples have a lot more sexual fun—which is also healthy for them—they are also more likely to develop much more of a sense of humor about the whole business of marriage. Their sexuality is also a reserve in the bank against other troubles in their relationship. Sexing couples have a place to go to "vacation" when things get rough. Quite obviously, these sexing couples beat the rap of their uptight and self-righteous cousins who so often end up sourpussy, dried out, and all-too-easily broken by the various other problems of marriage.

Affairs?

The symptomatic, quite-infrequent affair that says that one is testing one's machinery of protest and independence—best (for both spouses) to struggle to live with it even as you fight like hell to guard against it opening the door to an excess that would truly destroy any family unit!
The affair that is a cheap way out through repeated poking around everywhere but in the relationship of the marriage—stop this kind of cheating for sure, or else do indeed get out!

This one is going to be tough reading for a great many people.

On the other hand, it may be somewhat relieving for a few of those who happen to catch this material at a moment when they are caught up in their living hell of having discovered their spouse in an affair, although the worst of these moments hardly lend themselves to reading anything, this book included!

The Kinsey data of *many* years ago spelled out for us that a majority of men have some extramarital experience; and even then an amazingly large number of women did too.

There is every indication that both figures have swelled much higher by now. The pill made one of the big differences, of course. But there is also the unbelievable pace of social change otherwise—including the freeing of so much more of a fun-pleasure approach to sex in general. And so much more of an abandon about life as we see it to be oh-so-riddled-with-hell. And then too, a breakdown of so many fundamental values of our civilization including, to say the least, the profound deterioration in the whole structure of the family.

This is all so interesting a topic that we had best resolve not to go and devote ourselves to too many sides of the delicious topic of having affairs, or we shall lose our main focus. But we do have time for some poking about in this fun (and serious) matter.

First and foremost, we need to throw down some philosophical anchor about the relationship between affairs and the course of marriages.

There are some who preach a kind of free-and-easy attitude toward having fun with other mates. We say, swell, *if* that's the way it really can be for you. But we're skeptical about that, ourselves. In most instances, after the initial fun of discovery, we find that affairs, like all other human relationships, and certainly like all intimacies, become strained, complex struggles around the very kinds of complexities that mark the marital relationship. Time and time again, we have seen lovers getting into deep trouble because they begin to feel too many kinds of claims and demands for emotional relatedness from each other, rather than being able to leave it that theirs is the dalliance and jousting of fun, sport, and vacation.

There are those who turn to affairs with a kind of compulsive crudeness and greed and demand to have everything their own way on their terms all the time through life. We think the quality of these relationships speaks for itself. And the outcome should be pretty obvious too. Even the yield on the pseudosex is generally poor for all the boastful chest-beating. Though we might grant some animal fun of some good screws in this way, it's a tough life to integrate into family life for one or both partners.

And so we approach the more common instance which is that along the tricky, tough path of the marital relationship, there generally develop one or a few opportunities for that ultimate act of independence from one's spouse—that ultimate expression of revolt in the capacity to choose for one's self—making out with somebody else!

Here we'll start something really dangerous by revealing that many of these instances involve a close friend of the spouse!

The simplest explanation is that most of these instances involve a relatively close friend of the family whom one is seeing socially often enough to be able to build up that kind of momentum—let alone which enables people to find the opportunity to end up in bed together. Or on the floor.

(There is some deeper explanation too; but we will leave this as no more than a tantalizing suggestion for the reader to play with imaginatively.)

Of course, one should also add close business associates as a common target group. And especially someone with whom there is a relationship of some significant respect and mutual dependency in relation to shared tasks.

Anyway, most of these affairs last a very short time.

If this is so, is it really worth the marriage to blow one's cool and throw out either

a. the spouse,

b. the marriage,

or

c. one's self?

Hardly.

We disagree strongly with the sanctimonious mental-health tradition that conveys that the affair is a symptom of marital disturbance—as if to suggest that it doesn't happen among people who do not have seriously troubled or sick marriages.

We do agree that the affair is a sign and statement that it

is time for the marriage to go through one of its most dangerous tests; and this is indeed so troubled a period that often
people would benefit considerably by turning to professional
help at such a time—not because they are sick, but because
they are undergoing a serious crisis of development.

The affair means many things. Ultimately, it means a test
of the capacity of both spouses to bear an awareness of their
real separateness from one another; and a test of their capacity
to bear an awareness of the hatred of one another; and a test
of their capacity to bear an awareness of the evil potential of
one another; and with all this, to affirm a wish to be in union,
to have sex with each other more often than with anyone else,
to continue to build and deepen the family unit; always
clouded with doubt and fear and pain and hurt; but always
dignified by the awareness of choice reconfirmed under the
most difficult circumstances.

For our own sanity, each of us somehow must be able to
answer the question whether it really has to kill us if our
spouse unveils that private part and allows it to penetrate the
innards of another person? Really, it's a fun act that doesn't
have to have *all* that complicated meaning.

At least, it hardly seems worth one's life, does it?

CHAPTER FOURTEEN

THE KILLER ISSUES

II. WHEN TO DIVORCE

Does all that we've been saying mean staying with anything and everything?

Hell, no!

Let it be entirely clear that while we obviously encourage people to learn how to struggle from within themselves to discover the undreamt-of strengths of their marriage and themselves under all the stresses that develop, we do regard divorce as a natural right of people and support the removal of many of the arbitrary legal restrictions on divorce; and especially as they force spouses into adversary proceedings that call for blaming, lying, and bitterness in order to prove grounds for divorce.

The right to divorce should not be a judgment made by the State, but a judgment that each married person should be free to pursue—agonizedly, we hope, within himself.

At the same time, we would recommend that the legal process that is built around the arrangements for divorce convey in a variety of ways the dignity of the challenge of marriage, offer reminders of how much may be gained by triumphing over the adversity of the crisis, and provide an educational or counseling machinery to encourage people to discover what we have been describing all along—the hidden positives of pain and distress, and the funny universal game of it all, and the rewards of discovering yourself as far more lovable to yourself than you ever dreamed (all the while you were waiting for your spouse to love you as you thought you could not yourself).

So we would recommend that the process of divorce-seeking be mediated by marriage counselors from the outset.

Imagine, for example, marriage counselors acting as agents of the court and receiving the initial application for what might be considered "A Period of Contemplation of Divorce." Of course, the counselors would use these very application interviews to search out the possibilities of educating the applying couple to learn how to fight to improve their marriage. And the counselors would remain available to the couple during the mandatory Period of Contemplation.

We would even suggest that no lawyer be engaged by each spouse during this period; that there literally be no function for him, as there is now, where in effect the lawyer's financial interest in effecting the divorce must often influence his not being that committed to counseling for his client.

And insofar as an attorney may be needed at this early stage of first considering divorce, that this function be managed by legal officers of the court rather than an attorney to each of two adversaries.

Of course, the marriage counselor himself should have no stake in the outcome of the marriage other than his human interest in the people he is seeing and his hopes that they arrive at the best possible arrangement for them.

Over the Period of Contemplation, standard procedure would be that the couple be seen a number of times, and more frequently if they desired more intensive counseling. Say, a period of four months and eight counseling visits as standard. Both the time for cooling off and the experience of talking with a trained counselor would offer some relief of the original peak of passion of hatred, and some experience in getting out emotionally from one another.

If at the end of this period either member of the couple still felt the wish to divorce the other, legal machinery would then take up the process; now each spouse would turn to an attorney to act as his agent in leading him through the legal process, including arrangements through the court for equitable financial settlement with the spouse and for provision for any children of the marriage.

Were we serving as a marriage counselor in such a setup, what would be our position when it came to the question of when to divorce?

When divorce? If possible, only after one has exhausted as many alternatives as possible (and then some!), searching to find the meaningfulness that might be in a relationship even in the hell of it all. If possible, too, only at a point where one can conclude sadly that although much beauty there was and is in the other, too much stands in the way of the other person's coming to sufficient love for <u>himself</u> to be available to a working marriage at this time.

Notice the many points of difference in this kind of resolve from the traditional announcement of divorce.

"*I tried everything*," many people say quite sincerely; but we call for trying everything and then some.

Which will always mean professional help!

And which, in fact, would probably mean at least two such efforts if the first wasn't working out, so as to give one's self some assurance that it isn't faulty professional help, or even more simply the quality of the particular personality of the one counselor with a given couple that is holding the couple back.

And which would always mean a long period of time of struggle.

Our own experience in this regard is that knowing that one really has the emotional and moral right to divorce can provide a kind of strength for resolving to stay with the marital struggle for a goodly period of time (I would always use six months as my margin of resolve) before one need actually come to a decision; but feeling trapped, and "unable" to divorce, can understandably push people to a panic button of an impulsive and insistent decision when they hit a moment of passion in which they know that at that point they can somehow break out of bondage, but that they are not sure they could manage it at a later time.

The usual announcement of divorce also tends to present the other spouse as virtually anything but a human being. Each spouse recites tales of Inquisitional Hell by the other. Not that there shouldn't be plenty of rancor and hate and bitter accusations when a dream of marriage is shattered. There is nothing more unnatural than those seemingly mentally healthy situations of *friendly divorces* where people are oh-so-nice-and-friendly with each other as they go about ending something that "just didn't work out." Bullshit. It is an enormous loss when a marriage must be divorced. There has to be hurt anger. But one should also be able to remember the other spouse as the very one who once was the beloved person in one's life and who may still be quite attractive to him.

And why the divorce?

Not because the other won't give to me. Hurts me. Or hates me. It's not any of those—but because the other is unable to come to enough love of self to be able to give to me.

But how, how does one come to such a decision to divorce another who may still indeed be attractive to me?

Prayerfully!

Through lots of dream-study of one's self!

With much professional help examining the issue backward and forward, sideways and frontways!

And over a long period of time!

And then, with lots of luck indeed—to both of you!

But to flee into divorce as a kind of vindictive retaliation is to leave a legacy of bitterness and denial of one's own failure that will take a lifetime to ease.

Let's be blunt.

In many ways, unbearable tension does pass when one divorces one's self from a troubling marriage. Bachelors and spinsters really do have less heartache. But notice how eternally youthful, and childlike, so many of them seem. Even those with important positions in life. There is a kind of innocence on their face that one would like to think of as the bloom of health, and yet somehow, one senses more a kind of babylook of someone who doesn't really know what the score of life is. Someone who doesn't age properly. Like a good liquor does or a wizened sailor.

Yes, after divorce the tension is less. "I've never felt so good, ever since we broke up . . ." But let's be honest that this is the relief of being freed from the tension of the very contradictions through which the rest of us *may* be able to discover a deeper value of ourselves than we might ever be able to find were we on our own and away from such bitter tension.

Perhaps this may be one of the allegorical reasons Eve was formed *from* Adam; in our marriage to the *other*, it is ultimately our *own* self we may come to know in greater, rewarding depth as we are forced to turn back to our own deepest self when we find that the spouse on whom we would wish so much to depend cannot but fail us and drive us to virtual despair. Perhaps it is through this process that we are given an opportunity to discover further depths of the miracle of our own creation.

And what further rich allegory lies then in the natural truth that it is through this awesome struggle of two people to work together in marriage, even as they must end up discovering themselves because they cannot work together, that new lives are conceived, whom the embattled spouses are in turn charged with counseling and guiding how to find their own sense of value in a mad world, of which they are to be the shapers.

CHAPTER FIFTEEN

THE KILLER ISSUES

III. POWER PLAYING

TO CONTROL

THE OTHER

If marriage is a chance for *me* to discover *my* value as I thrust myself up against you as a sounding board and counter-force, then it follows that the worst you could do to me in our marriage would be to get in the way of my discovering myself.

By crowding me. (And me letting you crowd me.)

Invading me. (And me letting you invade me.)

Controlling me. (And me letting you control me.)

Getting inside of me. (And me letting you get inside of me.)

Note that all the above can be effected either in open brutality or *terribly* nicely. The meaning is the same. It is one person seeking his own meaning and value through forcible collections from the other.

It is emotional enslavement.

It is spouses seeking to possess one another—and then, how the flames of fear and rage burn should either spouse dare move toward loving life outside of the marriage!

It is the domination of another person's ideas—minimizing the other's mind, and lording it over him.

It is tyrannization of the other through a variety of sicknesses—some quite real perhaps but nonetheless *chosen:*

Mental illness. Suicide. I'll have a heart attack if you do such and such. Invalidism.

It is inducing guilt by being so nice, and decent, or weak and vulnerable—beware such meek and sweet who are really out to claim you in obligation unending to support them.

Over and over again, we see in the background of psychological disorder a feeling of being over-obligated to provide for another.

Over and over again, we see in the background of efforts to avoid psychological pain in one's self an effort to dominate another and make the other responsible for all.

Or, in the far more incredible, bizarre world of man's interpersonal relationships *out there,* in the big picture of life, we see human beings terrorizing each other unto literal deaths to little children, and helpless women, and non-combatant men— laughing madly as if in triumph over the essence of life, as if to say, "Now, I shall never have to worry about my own lacks, for I have demonstrated that I can control Life itself!"

To be a decent and healthy human being, one need neither invade another nor be invaded.

Do your own thing. Your spouse is not you and you are not your spouse. "Knock before entering each other."

Don't claim all as coming to you.

And don't be claimed as owed to another.

Be you.

And help the other be him.

Meet occasionally to share your selves, but always return to your own self.

It is the subtleties of power-playing that are the most ominous and also of greatest interest.

Openly tyrannical people are relatively easy to oppose. And of those poor souls—alas, too numerous—who settle for such, it can at least be said that in all conscious senses of the word, they know what they are getting.

It is the nice-looking, everyday-appearing people—like all of us—who are out to keep control of much of their spouse's being that are the more difficult to look at and contend with.

In fact, since all of us human beings are disastrously incomplete, and especially in our youths glaringly lacking in one or more areas of personal development and skills for life; and since the notion that one can get what one wants by overpowering another who possesses same springs all too readily to the human mind; many, many marital relationships start out with quite a lot of subtle, powerful power-plays at gaining what one lacks from the other by controlling the spouse to produce these missing "goods."

Thus:

You be smart for me—as I do not feel adequate in my intelligence.

You be beautiful for me—as I fear I am unattractive.

You be dutiful for me—as I fear I cannot command another's enduring love or loyalty.

And so forth.

Insofar as these are demands to control the other—rather than requests, or simply needs with which one hopes to have the other's help—the demands are generally backed by pretty powerful sanctions and threats of punishment where it's likely to hurt the other the most.

Basically, the retaliating threat is some version or another of—

Or else I won't love you!

Better yet—

Or else I'll leave you!

The human mind being infinitely clever, this power-play is generally further adjusted precisely to the specifics of where it is that the other feels least able to stand being left alone.

In fact, since 'tis a two-party association to begin with that

the marital contract concerns, and what we said about the
human tendency to press the other to supply one's lacks concerns both partners to the arrangement, power-playing arrangements generally involve a simultaneous trade-off of attempts to control one another. And the best way to leave the
other for failure to produce as demanded is to leave the other
high and dry on their most basic contract stipulation, that is,
where the spouse of the second part needs the most from the
spouse of the first part.

So we are likely to be dealing with two-way contracts that
go like this:

SPOUSE 1 TO SPOUSE 2	SPOUSE 2 TO SPOUSE 1
Be independent <u>for me</u>	*Reassure me of your total availability <u>for me</u>*
or else	*or else*
I will not provide for you.	*I will not provide for you.*

No doubt it will not have been lost on the reader that in
addition to setting up a trade-off of *I'll leave you where you
need the most unless you do my bidding,* the example we just
created was purposely constructed around an exchange of opposite or complementary qualities so that the spouse who
provides for the couple a quality of independence from the
pressures and demands of others—say, other family, as one
frequent example in life—simultaneously demands of the other
a huge quantity of reassuring dependency; or phrased from
the other side, the spouse who is the big provider of tranquil-
izing over-security demands of the other protection from having to face the needs and demands of people in other relationships.

It will be recalled that we were talking about such complementarity in an earlier chapter of our "first book." Along
with a fair number of other psychological observers of family
life, we have a hunch that *many* marriages, especially those

that grow from that most marvelous of dimly understood "psychoatomic reactions" of falling deeply in love, build unconsciously around such trade-offs of complementary qualities, and, even more, as we wrote in the earlier section, trade-offs of complementary qualities that in themselves often carry the tension of still further inner complementarity.

Thus:

SPOUSE 1 TO SPOUSE 2	SPOUSE 2 TO SPOUSE 1
I will be totally available for you— *so long as you allow me to attach myself to your independence,* *because I am afraid of how much* *I need to assert my independence*	*I will be independent for you—* *so long as you are totally available to me,* *because I am afraid of how dependent I do (would) feel inwardly*

The naturalistic point of all this is that it is tapping the ferment—the energy-releasing explosions of these complex interchanges that gives us all both incredible troubles and also great chances for growing in our marriages.

The real problem is that few of us know how to do such growing; let alone that for the most part we have no idea what a complex process we are headed into when we marry.

Our main point here, though, is that much of the trouble comes from people trying to *force* the other to do their bidding, rather than entering into a cooperative volunteer contract in which there will be an effort to exchange *helpful services* with one another.

For the attempt to force the other means by definition that I will not be making an effort to reduce my undue need for you in the area of my weakness and limitation; and that I shall be resisting trying to grow for myself; and if you ever dare grow out of providing for me in this area of my neediness, then I am doomed—and I will have to fight back as only the doomed do.

That's setting up murderous trouble.

What is the near-absurdity of it all, we think, is that our understanding at this point is that most of us, if not virtually all of us, quite naturally and necessarily go into marriage on just these bases. The challenge is to grow out of this arrangement to negotiate a new contract some years later in the marriage.

Who of us is complete enough not to need another desperately at that point in our development when we are first climbing to the next rung on the ladder of life that is marriage?

And how many of us have been fortunate enough by then to have learned a model of being with and exchanging helpfulness with another without placing ourselves at the mercy of an absolute requirement of the other's help (as well as not playing into accepting the other's placing such a burden on us)?

Of course, it is somewhat useful to think of how people line up differently in their maturities for marriage before the fact; but it is at least just as useful to then think of how well or not they do in responding to the challenge of growing that is marriage.

To come together in intimacy;
And to separate from needing each other so *much.*

Dear Spouse,
Please join me in living together—I for myself,
and you for yourself. Whereupon it becomes much fun
to see and be with another person living through the
same experiences—of becoming more of a person. And
I shall enjoy helping you as best I can—And I need your
help so very much—But not so desperately for either
of us that we can't make it for ourselves alone—Which,
ultimately, in a deep sense is where we all are.

What this means, when there are the inevitable conflicts to live through, is that the two spouses need to work together to find ways for *both* to win!

In recent years, we have been hearing of a new concept of human relations that is being called a *no-lose* approach.

In international relations this means the intent of the international negotiators on both sides is to develop solutions that meet the needs of both peoples, not to hammer across their negotiating demands competitively.

And in parent-child relations: It is not parents winning over kids (they don't); nor children running parents; but a creative dialogue of emotional equals seeking a spirit of *all-win* in the family.

No-lose means yielding the search for personal power in favor of mutual power!

It is not a washing-out compromising between two people, for it involves the full measure of each human being's deepest thrust for himself and his needs.

Nor is it taking turns—I'll scratch your back this time, and you'll scratch mine next.

And it is not postponing an issue so nobody need lose face.

It is the creative press of two people knowing that real human needs honor one another; that it is nature's way to reconcile the irreconcilable in greater new wholes.

That two people have so much more to gain as they press to find how genuinely to ζ et the needs of both.

Like in sex!

And in marriage overall—to the extent we are clever enough to find how to build a *both-way* process.

Power to all of us to play the game of life as a more fun thing!

CHAPTER SIXTEEN

COMMITMENT TO ONE'S MARRIAGE—

A WAY TO GET THE MOST

FOR ONE'S SELF

Now we are nearing the end of the trail we have set for ourselves to think out more creatively how to get on with *living* in our trouble-full marriages.

For one's own sake, above all, though, also in a very special way for the sake of one's children, and to a smaller extent even a bit for one's spouse, it is good to commit one's self to stay with one's marriage—if at all possible!

There is a real value to contracts. They offer a framework of some security against rashly impulsive blowing up of relationships.

Contracts also are a reminder that another period of negotiation for renewal of the contract will be coming up. Which means that you mind your p's and q's—they're all precedents. And which certainly means that we're not wedded to each other forever—just if we decide to continue being wed the next time around.

So—"contractual" commitment to one's marriage offers a sense of security and meaning to one's self and one's family, especially when the going gets rough, as it always does.

And then comes the surprising discovery: that the very commitment makes one feel good and clean about doing one's best, with the further result that one is so much stronger for coping with problems than he might have been.

To commit one's self to a marriage means a commitment to find our *own* deepest resources; often, we then make a surprising discovery that we have in us so much more strength than we ever dared dream about. It is precisely when we discover that our spouse is utterly, ruthlessly unreliable and will never take care of us as we had hoped, that we face the possibility of running . . . or discovering new fountains of coping-capacity and self-love within ourselves.

Not a bad deal, when you think about it.

You "lose" a spouse. But gain yourself! And because you were willing to stay and fight for something better, from deeper in yourself, when your spouse finked out, rather than pick up your poker chips and run into the comfort of protesting how lousy your spouse was.

How good it is to love one's self.
Yet, how utterly impossible it is to love one's self
enough.
How much will I feel better if you love me and care for
me.
Yet, sadly I discover you will never do for me as I
hoped you would.
In fact, often you will hurt me!
You even seek to destroy me!
God, I need myself; but there is not enough of me!
God, I need you; but there is too little good from you!
I need both, don't I? Myself, in all my failings, and
then you, too, in all your failings!
Each time you fail me, I go back to discovering more
of myself and feel stronger.
Each time I am far from enough for myself, I return to
seek you; and when I find you, I am so grateful for you
just as you are.

God, how I love myself and hate myself!
God, how I love you and hate you!
How agonizing the never-ending contradictions!

Suddenly, I feel calmer.
How ingenious this life process of contradiction press-
ing against contradiction—always swirling, always
generating, always pushing me toward
an awe of life itself.
Of which I am a beautiful part!

CHAPTER SEVENTEEN

LOVE (hate)!

It is time to put in a stronger word for the love side of the equation.

We think that we've been conveying fairly interestingly and fully that the hate in the relationship isn't all that bad, that it is another aspect of being in a relationship which is in effect a form of loving; that anyway it is, and since you can't fight it, by all means join it.

However, notwithstanding our use of the introduction to make it entirely clear that our intent is entirely on the side of building a more satisfying intimacy in marriage, we are concerned that in our enthusiasm for the newer task of respecting and loving the hating, we may well have neglected the staid, old-fashioned job of affirming that love of the positive sort is really very, very good and necessary stuff.

It is so important that we be sure to convey a picture of the marital potential as grown of an equation that integrates love and hate as two inseparable sides of an authentic, genuine— non-power-playing—relationship.

Since to our everyday minds love and hate seem so different, and since the one side of the authentic totality, hate, is by far less well understood, we have been concentrating on teaching healthy hating.

So this note late in the book is a caution that we remember old-fashioned love is indeed an irreplacable core of the (loving and hating) effort at relationship with another.

This point is easy to make, of course:

Love!
Yes, care and treasure and help the other!
Free people enjoy loving!

We suppose all we need say is that all that man has said through the ages about the importance of loving one's spouse and the importance of caring for the other person is entirely true.

Every word of the minister, priest, and rabbi.

And every word of the modern marriage counselor and psychologist speaking of maturity and understanding and caring for the wife or husband.

Love does need to triumph over hate.

There should be restraint of anger.

We do need to protect our spouses from their weaknesses.

And we do need to protect the children from being caught between us, or being allowed to divide us.

All true—*to a point.*

The *only* trouble has been that all this mature loving plain doesn't work *by itself.*

And that's why we went looking for the other element, the catalyst/ the trigger/ the partner in the energy process; that's how we came to discover that the very force that crops up all the time when people try to love each other, hate, really has its place: to release people's hurt, to vent the buildup of angry heat, to provide a vehicle for genuine criticism of the other, to provide for separateness of two equal people, in effect, to clear a path for all the loving we would wish to feel.

Perhaps it is something comparable to the constructive hurting and cutting of the dentist's drill and the surgeon's knife.

Or might we think of excavating to clear the way for building a house?

But tearing away alone will build neither a healthy person nor a house, and that's very much the story in the marriage process.

More on the loving itself, we think we need not speak that much. People tend to know how to love fairly easily once they (are free to) put themselves to it. And in any case there are many beautiful guides to loving through all the ages.

However, to love *and* hate, that's another matter.

Someday, we hope there will be new guides in a new language that knows how to say what we are now laboring so to put together:

>LOVE (*hate*)

And when you must, as must 'twill be many times.

>HATE (*love*)

Although at any given time the latter will take precedence —given two equal trainloads of love and hate coming through, the emotional rules seem to give the hate (love) trainload precedence in time—nonetheless, try overall to have it that you

>LOVE (*hate*) *more than you* HATE (*love*).

CHAPTER EIGHTEEN

MARITAL LOVE AND HATE
IN THE PRESENCE OF
AND CONCERNING
THE CHILDREN

Never fight in front of the children? On the contrary, fight fairly often in front of the children! (Deal them in on some of the good stuff of fights!) But fight wisely and well!

It is easy to understand the well-intentioned efforts of so many people to put away their fights in front of the kids.

Children *do* become upset by parental anger; characteristically, children experience themselves as the *cause* of parental arguing; in the chronically angry family, and in the family that succumbs to divorce, children inevitably experience themselves unconsciously as the cause of their parents' failure. Sc one would indeed think that it would be best to spare children from carrying this burden.

The fact is, however, that not only is it a virtual impossibility not to have fights that the kids will become aware of, but children would lose out on a very necessary kind of vaccination for themselves if they were indeed entirely protected from seeing parental fighting. Consider the very issue of the children feeling that they are responsible for their parents' dissension; how good to give them a sequence of experiences in which they find that fights are followed by—and in effect represent part of a sequence of—caring and contact and commitment to one another; what a fine answer that is to their feelings of responsibility!

Besides, take a long range point of view, and children who do not see good parental fighting in their own growing-up homes will be ill-prepared for their own future marital fights; let alone, it is at home that they might learn so much of how they might seek a position of dear, nonviolent strength for all their living in this mad world.

It is now a demonstrated fact in research on creativity that children from homes in which differences are experienced openly between parents tend notably to be more creative than children from homes where there is a guiding kind of uniformity or party-line solidarity.

The trick is not to put anger away so much as to show the children that when anger is experienced, it does not destroy either party, it is not acted out in overt violence, it is not carried to irrational extremes (at least not always, only sometimes, and then with notable recoverability following); and to let the children see that out of the parents' respect for their children, to whom they are both loyal, the parents do indeed put aside their more regressive fighting behaviors for moments of their greater privacy (of which the children will of course get just enough intimation to know what is going on without having been exposed to it).

The trick is to see and learn good, clean fighting.

And fight about the children! In fact, be thoroughly sure that any child who tends to receive a raw deal from one of you parents has his other parent squarely in his camp, fighting against the raw-dealing mother or father quite openly!

The least that will happen is that it will break up the automatic repetitions of the raw deal. And it makes perfectly good sense that kids who get a raw deal regularly from a parent without intervention or help of any sort get to feel inside of themselves pretty darn undeserving and unlovable as people —this over and above the raw deal that they already are getting as such.

Put the other parent in their camp as their champion, and as a fighter for fairness, and you introduce at least the possibility of the child emerging with a sense of being lovable and deserving enough that he won himself one ally.

Besides, there is frequently the chance that the second parent's intervention will in fact stop the repetitive raw deal from happening. For it is certainly true over and over again in human affairs that many mothers or fathers, and human beings in many other life contexts other than parenting, get to being terrifyingly lousy to someone, but all the while they are hoping against hope that either their victim or another person on the scene will come along to stop them from their lousiness which, after all, ultimately eats away at their own sense of decency.

In addition, this very process of intervention on behalf of the beaten-on child will set off that whole process of marital relating about which we have been talking; and the youngster who may indeed be quite hurt by the raw deal he is getting from the one parent, and also guilty for "causing" all the marital strife, may at least end up reaping the benefits of being witness to, and therefore learner from, the honesty and courageousness and equality of his parents if they can fight it out constructively.

We believe the arithmetic of it is that the son of a father who gives him a hard time without his mother standing up to his father will come out of it more hurt than the son of the same rough father whose mother would courageously stand up to her husband and call him on his unfairness.

Sounds lightly amusing as a seeming matter of family arithmetic, but, in fact, it is far more than a laughing matter. When we study the various kinds of serious developmental distortions that affect children and young people, it turns out that although the clustering of parental influences and forces that characteristically shape each disorder vary (e.g., the homosexual young man characteristically is dominated by his mother and in a way where he chooses to surrender to her domination without conscious protest; e.g., the behavior-disordered child in most cases is unconsciously encouraged to act out for one of his parents), *virtually all situations of emotional disorder in children have in common the fact that the other parent did not take active efforts to challenge, limit, and fight back against that particular damaging quality in the more stage-center parent that psychological study leads us to identify in a focal way with the subsequent emotional or character defect of the young person.*

Take the autistic child who was abandoned by his attractive, intelligent mother to hours of being alone except for times of largely mechanical, proper care; and even if there were some hours of some real affection, nonetheless these were isolated islands in a larger sea of being ignored to himself.

What might have been had the father demanded irately that there be more contact between his wife and child?

What might be the outcome to a turned-off child if a husband of a quarrelsome, pushy, critical, perfectionistic mother told her to shut up, and to lay off?

And the child who grows up sad and hungry for care because mother packaged him into her routines of club work and housekeeping, and doing things, but not relating to the person that each child is. What would be had his father called the shots as they were happening and insisted that his wife really *be* with their child?

And the boy who grows up in violent hatred of his tyrannical father—a pompous, egotistical, icily controlling man. How might he fare were his mother other than "sweetly" retiring and compromising, and were she able to stand up to her husband to cut him down to the size that all men are?

Recently, I gave a graduate class in special education an assignment to describe a distorted parent-child relationship; their assignment was first to focus on the *essential distortion* of what the parent was "after" in the troubled relationship with the child, and then the students were further instructed as follows: "Also, be sure to add at the end a single, clear statement of how the other parent related or reacted to the distorted behavior of the parent you are describing."

Fascinatingly enough, the group divided reasonably equally in presenting situations where the key villain in the troubled parent-child relationship was a mother versus situations where it was papa who was the monster; but *in every case*, without exception, the concluding observation about the other spouse was that spouse B copped out and failed to engage in real criticism of the villain, or in any sustained effort to protest or retaliate, or in any way correct the erring parent.

In short, the one parent was the criminal, but the other parent was the accomplice—sometimes to first-degree stuff. Thus a situation where the mother was constantly leaving her family, and the student wrote of the other:

> The father reacted to the situation with submission; because of his love for his wife he seemed willing to sacrifice the emotional well-being of his children although he seemed to love them very much.

Horseshit that he *loved* his wife! We can safely infer that the truth was he was terrified of her. How many spouses are so terrified of taking a stand, speaking their minds; so often, the all-consuming fear is that if one is open in opposition to the spouse, the latter will leave; and it is on this altar that so many children's needs are sacrificed. We might trust the observation of the student that the father loved his kids, but genuine as his love might have been, it was too weak to be a stimulus to actions of greater courage.

Another instance was reported by a student of a boy who was smothered by his mother.

> The father of this boy tried at first to intercede in this relationship. He met only opposition from his wife, and soon his attempts were causing a very strained relationship between him and his wife. Now he just turns his back on the whole situation and never interferes.

So too on the other side of the Adam and Eve scoreboard, a student reported a case of a father who became extremely jealous of any boy who was the least interested in his daughter. The student reporting this incident was the girl in question. She describes how:

> This came to the point of the ridiculous when I was a senior in college, age 21, and he told me that *he* had decided that I could have friends, but no serious boyfriends.

About the spouse here.

> My mother is a very determined woman, but she has just given up. We were never really that close to start out with. She is sympathetic, but just shrugs her shoulders and says to ignore it.

Another student described a father who had no respect for his children at all; he thought of and treated them as something subhuman. Anytime there was any kind of natural need for recognition by one of the children, the father took it as a personal threat.

And here the spouse:

> The mother, who had been treated the same as the children, reacted as an indifferent pacifier. If she allowed the father to see that his verbal lashings hurt her also, the

father would use the situation to its fullest, and treat the boy worse!

By now, we know all too well how hard it is in too many instances to reverse the powerful lifelong effects of many a serious problem in a person's childhood.

The symptoms through which people pay a high price are legion: be it a disturbed child who is being seen in treatment; or the failing adult that was once a child; be the patient "schizophrenically" out of it; or neurotically anxious about it all; or phobically avoiding one situation or another of the risks of life; or a learning-problem child who has given up those most natural qualities of discovering and experiencing that are what we mean by learning; be it an overly aggressive, defiant, rebellious personality; or a bed-wetter, thumb-sucker, screwer of or by animals, impotent in this limb or that limb, unable to control or master the joyful use of this natural function or that one; in all of these many and varied instances we have learned only too well to reconstruct a characteristic childhood picture of a kind of invasion of the inherent dignity or being of the now-suffering patient.

Consider the sheer magic of reduction of human suffering that might be if in the face of such invasion and exploitation of a child by a parent there were the other parent—that is, every one of us who is an *other* to *another!*—to get in there and take a stand and intervene.

Admittedly, this would leave scarred the smaller number of kids whose two parents were fully in tune with one another in their eating up the child's spirit.

But every little bit of improvement of the human condition helps. All of which is deeply related to the issue of a Kitty Genovese incident—where, dear readers, you will recall, a young woman was killed in New York in full view of some forty people, and not a single one of them went to her aid or even called the police!

The world has seen, and is seeing, its full of situations of individual or mass murder where there are not only the killers themselves in all the depravity of their doing, but also the countless human beings who are accomplices to the act; some directly indeed; but also so, so many who are the accomplices by way of being indifferent bystanders who feign unconsciousness of what is happening, or who go so far in self-protection as to induce a real amnesic inability to be conscious of that which is passing before their perfectly healthy eyes or is bursting against their perfectly intact eardrums.

Perhaps then there is a larger meaning to the family triangle we have been describing where there is the oppressor parent and victim child, and another parent as witness. Perhaps this family situation—we would suggest it is one where all of us parents are drawn often enough to both types of role, although we probably favor one more than the other—is also a training ground or proving ground for one's capacity to take a stand among the larger family of man where we must take a stand on all too many situations of invasion of one people by another, and disrespect and domination, and exploitation—to the point of death-dealing attacks that are quite literal.

Personally, I'd fight my spouse's indifference to genocide going on around us.

And I believe it only right that I fight my spouse on injustices to our own children.

And I pray she stop me from my madnesses.

CHAPTER NINETEEN

WHEN ALL ELSE FAILS

REMAIN

AN ATTRACTIVE PERSON

It is with great sadness that we must now acknowledge that most of the preceding list of principles for survival in the inferno are of dubious value, and even those that have some meaning are quite limited in their effectiveness!

For the truth is, that the process is so complex, that every little piece that we glimpse means that the rest is bouncing away from us, laughing uproariously as it were, and preparing to hurtle back at us in strange new forms as if life itself is an infinity of masquerades, thrusting and meteoric, and tantalizing the hell out of us.

Now you see it, now you don't!

Move along folks, move along; there's room for everybody!

We're all on a merry-go-round in space itself. An unfathomable space of galaxies of galaxies.

It has been conjectured that somewhere out there there are creatures who might be entirely like us except for the one fundamental quality that their chemistry is exactly antithetical to ours, meaning in the language of our physics that each of us would represent anti-matter to the other; so that when we would go to shake hands, poof . . . ! we would disintegrate each other!

Often I am drawn to the fantasy that there are little particles of such anti-matter residing in every spouse coupling away on our own little earth planet, that this is something that makes for that "molecular excitement" that marks the falling in love of us critters who choose each other in such a flash of excitement that will soon be generating such enormously troubling, perplexing confusion.

So, it's really doubtful as hell that whatever we seem to know in this book is particularly knowable!

Under these sad circumstances, it seems only right that we leave our gentle reader with a final emergency hatch. And this is it:

Remain Attractive!

Don't get too angry.
Don't get too fat.
Don't let your sexing go get stale.
Don't stop learning.
Don't stop having a sense of humor about life itself. And certainly about yourself.
Be fun.
The kind of person dogs like.
And kids.
And you, yourself.
And then, no matter what happens, whether your spouse dies, divorces you, makes life eighty percent miserable, disappears, gets silly, the stock market crashes, your business or professional associates leave you, your kids convert to another religion, your religion converts to principles, the wrong man gets elected President, your airplane develops engine trouble, your grass doesn't grow well—and you know that whole list —you'll at least have—

Yourself!

Oh, about being attractive—sometimes,
when you don't feel it,
don't hesitate to

BLUFF IT!

a final perspective:

MARRIAGE IS A SMALL-SCALE BATTLE-

GROUND OF MAN'S CHOICES

OF WAR OR PEACE

A final thought for twentieth-century couples: In our marriages each of us is given a chance to participate in a worldwide and mankind-wide panorama of choices as to whether or not each man will allow his aggressiveness to mount into destructive, warring forms, or whether each of us will learn to feel angry and aggressive in *feelings* but not in violent destructive *action*.

In each marriage the choice is not between happiness and unhappiness, but between a respectful, cooperative state of nonviolent tension, where quite often we must experience anger though often we may also enjoy a more positive, empathizing love; or a state of increasingly violent, demoralizing, depersonalizing destruction of one or another. And so it is in all of our universe that we must face as collective groups of people learning how to live with our differences, expecting there will be disagreements all the time, and much anger, but learning how to create a lawful machinery for the expression and resolution of these differences, rather than succumbing to the age-old impulses to destroy and be destroyed.

POSTSCRIPT

For a book that is all about love and hate,
it seems only right to be aware from the
outset that a lot of people are going to
love and hate this book—and in quite varied ways.

Word of this kind of thing—
that someone is talking about the inevitability
of trouble in marriage,
and how one might beat the system by joining it—
gets out fast, needless to say.

> (Unhappily, this has nothing to do with the value
> of any of the ideas,
> much like the unfortunate observation
> that how much business a doctor has
> is not at all necessarily correlated with
> the doctor's competence.)

> Appearance of the original statement of this work in
> the professional journal, *Family Process*, elicited
> a wide variety of responses, loving, middling, and
> you-know-what!

We bring here a sampling of some of the loving
and hating reactions to different parts of the
work, or to the basic concern with loving and
hating, that have already come our way.

We are also appending a couple of therapy-
derived case illustrations that speak interestingly
to the mysteries we are probing of when hate is
too much and when loving is too much.

INTELLIGENCE REPORT *

**Fight and
enjoy it**

The process of living is no bed of roses, never has been and never will be. And it isn't realistic or particularly helpful to exempt marriage from this viewpoint.

Modern explorers of the psychotherapy of marriage offer enlightened observations on coping with difficulties.

But for Dr. Israel W. Charny of Paoli, Pa., these are only half truths.

Charny believes that the conflict in marriage is not only inevitable, but also desirable. Those unions marked by conflicts are not the unfortunate few, but the common many. There is nothing wrong with this. Like aggression, conflict can be expressed either destructively or constructively.

Charny lists some constructive suggestions about marital fighting and loving in a recent issue of *Family Process* magazine:

"It is natural and right to feel anger.

"It is very much wrong to hurt another person, overtly, in *acts* against the other's person, but to *feel* like hurting another is a natural expression of anger.

"Feelings are not the same as actions; our feelings of anger in no way really punish or hurt the other party in a literal sense."

Charny emphasizes the need to distinguish between feelings and actions. He also has firm notions about fighting in front of children.

Since Charny sees anger as natural and fighting as a necessary means of expression, he favors allowing children to view this process.

* from *Parade, The Sunday Newspaper Magazine*, June 29, 1969.

There is, as Ecclesiastes puts it, "a time to love and a time to hate." A study of murders between spouses reveals that the murderers are often those who are least able to express their anger on a reasonable level, finally explode into a murderous battle. Fighting, says Charny, is "inevitable and necessary and desirable—simply not a byproduct of emotional immaturity or disturbance."

Dr. Charny concurs with other current research which contends that violence is an outdated method of coping in our technological society. If we wish to survive, with some ability to form unions between people, as individuals or nations, we must learn to express and channel aggressions nonviolently.

A reporter for the VOICE OF AMERICA came a'calling and developed a delightful interview which I could then fantasy would be reaching into igloos, camel tents, and a variety of alluring shacking-up places.

This was fun.

The same lady reporter had a husband who worked the other end of the media street selling magazine articles. When wife reporter requested for her husband the right to write up the radio interview, I agreed, though with a gentleman's understanding that I would be able to preview the writeup.

So it was done.

One day shortly afterwards, a fairly similar version of the interview appeared in a weekly newspaper, the NATIONAL ENQUIRER—under a byline of a man I had never met, who is not the lady's husband, along with a posed photo of family fighting I had never seen, and of all places right across from a page spread that announced singer Eddie Fisher's determination never to marry again!

Prominent Psychologist Says . . .
Fighting Can Help a Marriage If
The Partners Know How to Argue*

A fight with your husband or wife can be constructive, healthy, good for the children and good for your marriage —if you know how to handle your arguments and what to avoid during marital quarrels.

The rules of "fair fighting" are simple, according to Dr. Israel W. Charny of Pennsylvania, who said:

"A lot of fighting in front of kids is good. But fighting about sex in front of kids, that's dirty pool.

"Feeling like hitting one another, that's very natural,

and can be said, such as: 'I feel like killing you. I wish you were dead,' but hitting another person, that is wrong.

"When you live with somebody who is a yes-man or a yes-gal, all the mistakes that every one of us makes will never get challenged. It will never be called to your attention that you may be smug or bored or arrogant and you are not challenged to try to become a better person.

"One of the constructive ways to fight is by saying to yourself: 'Okay, a fight is a chance for me to say things I really feel to this other person I am living with, and the fight is a chance for me to hear some of the real truths about me from another person.' "

Dr. Charny is a member of the American Board of Professional Psychology, a clinical psychologist practicing in Paoli, Pa., where he directs a private group practice, Guidance Consultants, and is coordinator of a research group in the psychology of aggression and nonviolence. He believes that since fighting among married couples is inevitable, it should be made helpful.

He said: "It is inevitable because the very business of living together closely has to bring an awful lot of rough edges up for both people. Since there is so much that forces differences to the surface, take a leap and think to yourself that, well, maybe it is desirable that these differences are here."

Dr. Charny said that one of the most important things to remember is that "all marital fighting is dirty and below the belt and therefore should never be taken at face value."

He explained: "Fighting should be taken like a fable, a symbol of what you and the other person are saying. Listen, and listen quietly, and you'll hear the truth of your own unfairness or selfishness."

A couple that knows how to fight well, Dr. Charny said, knows that an argument is not won "when one person surrenders his sword to the other and says: 'You were right, oh wise one, and I was wrong, forgive me!'

"As a matter of fact, never expect your opponent to agree openly. Watch for the cues that say both of you have said what you really feel, and then turn it off, take off, do something else."

The psychologist believes that people who fight generally love more than those who repress themselves.

He said: "Lots of people have sensed that, and there are all sorts of folk observations that nothing is so delicious as the loving that follows a lovers' quarrel.

"Actually, in a deeply subtle way, it seems that the capacity to fight and the capacity to love really are two sides of the same essential thing, and that essential thing is the capacity to be yourself in a real way with another human being."

According to Dr. Charny, fighting fairly in front of children will teach them how to be better husbands and wives in the future, so long as the fight is not about sex.

This, he said, is "too overstimulating for the children and it becomes confusing for the adults themselves.

"If fighting is lousy and destructive," he explained, "a youngster will get very upset and guilty and feel in some way responsible for it.

"This certainly is a theme that comes out over and over again in kids where marriages break up.

"But if the fighting in the house is fair, children generally show a kind of release and joy after a good parental battle."

An important rule stressed by Dr. Charny is for couples never to take their own words literally, such as when one of the quarrelers says he is fed up and feels like getting a divorce.

"Understand that the feeling is real. It really is.

"There isn't a couple alive who doesn't feel at some time like getting a divorce.

"But you don't have to treat the words literally. I would hate to count the number of couples who got divorced because somebody uttered the words and neither partner knew how to treat this as a feeling, rather than a fact."

Dr. Charny was asked if there is any time limitation on fighting in marriage, once a day or once a week.

He said: "No one has gotten statistics on that accurately, so maybe, for the moment, we should just leave it as comparable to the statistics on sexual relations."

He said that if fighting in marriage doesn't improve the marriage, then the couples should go to a professional counselor to learn how to make the fighting help them, rather than turn them into enemies, since they obviously do not understand how to conduct a fair fight.

Dr. Charny also said he is married, "and yes, we fight."

Waitress (smiling) in a restaurant the next day:

"I read your article in the paper. It was very interesting. I agree with you a lot. But [somehow conveying she means the part about fighting in front of the kids] I don't agree with you about everything."

One of the men in my favorite hardware store:

"Hey, Doc [leering], I saw you all over the *National Enquirer*. How did you get into that paper? And I don't know about some of your ideas [somehow conveying his assurance of a greater dignity in his family life]. It was pretty interesting reading, but there's a lot I don't agree with you about."

A patient sent me a photocopy with just this note:
  "The National Enquirer????!!!!"

Most valuable of all was a mini-review that "Marital love and hate" elicited from an able colleague, one who has the unusual distinction of working along with his wife-psychologist as pioneers of public psychological education through radio and TV shows that takes peoples' questions as they come in, *where they're at*, and offer thoughtful, professional comments for all of the stress of the immediate "entertainment moment." The Drs. Bricklin are also established authors of both scientific and popularly oriented works.

It was fun to see that Dr. B.B. was troubled enough by "Marital love and hate" to feel a need to write an unsolicited criticism—and that he even needed to reach for that old getter-together, "We're really after the same aims . . ."

But he disagrees. And it only seems right to postscript our work on love and hate with a good solid criticism (permission to print same is greatly appreciated).

August 14, 1969

Dr. Israel W. Charny
Station Square One
Paoli, Pennsylvania 19301

Dear Is:

Thank you for sending me your paper on *Marital Love and Hate*. As usual, it is interestingly written, well prepared, thought-provoking, and lively.

However, I am not very sympathetic to the let's-teach-'em-to fight school for several reasons.

1. Arguing is not the same thing as a chronic blaming hostility, and the two are easily confused. The latter would seem to involve self-hatred and some sort of deep-set belief that it is terrible to be personally blamed for anything —that one must at all costs direct this blame at someone else.

2. No matter the school of therapy to which one subscribes, it would seem that the real culprit in producing

symptoms and ineffective behavior is self-hatred, no matter what it may be called in the various systems. I fear
that nothing genuine is purchased by the teach-the-mates-
to-fight-school except the externalization of self-hatred
(i.e., a breathing spell purchased at someone else's expense). The real job is to reduce the self-hatred.

3. In essence, your advice seems to be that he who is
healthy is he who has a commitment *to solve, not to blame*
problems as they arise, and not waste time thinking one
can ever reach a stage where there are no problems (as
some irrationally expect from a certain stage in marriage).
This advice would include that people should not waste
time bitching about how things are not like they would
like them to be. It is this *commitment* which defines mental health rather than how angry a person happens to be
at one time or another. I agree that anger and aggression
are genuine parts of us. However, I think it is the *commitment to deal with them at no one's expense (including
one's own)* that is the important element in producing a
therapeutic victory. One can sense when a person achieves
this commitment. It is unrelated to the presence or absence of overt aggression.

4. The main reason for my lack of sympathy to the new
wave of books teaching mates to fight is that the whole
thing seems phony. By the time the various authors get
done defining aggression it is no longer aggression. It has
been so detoxified by various definitional necessities on
how one may properly fight that it is no longer the genuine
article. It is like the difference in emotion felt by wrestlers
as opposed to boxers—in the latter case the hatred is real,
while in the former largely detoxified.

5. The teach-'em-to-fight books do help, however, in
an indirect sort of way. By this I mean that the sanction
to fight has already reduced self-hatred to some extent and
so the real battle is won before the marital fight even takes
place. By the time one has made all the recommended
distinctions e.g., enjoy your partner's life force as mani-
fested in her aggression, etc., the anger is already neu-

tralized and not experienced as an attack. It has been changed by prior definition. My concern is that people will remember the titles of these different books but not learn how to really use them.

In short, I am unconvinced. I still believe it is necessary to reduce *irrational* anger. (Refer to our book *Strong Family—Strong Child*, N.Y.: Delacorte, 1970, for the distinction.) There are enough instances of rational aggression in the world without having to add irrational anger. I also believe that a blaming type of anger makes all communication, even the communication of (differentiated) emotions impossible. When one feels blame emanating from someone else, one erects a wall through which nothing penetrates. I cannot see this as a positive asset.

Nevertheless, I certainly agree it is foolish to lead people to believe therapists expect them magically to become non-aggressive overnight, or that it is possible to live without at least some anger on many occasions, and intense, explosive anger on others. If the teach-'em-to-fight books accomplish anything, they seem to do so by making people feel less guilty and self-hating, when they *do* get angry. In this way it is quite possible these same individuals feel ever so slightly *less* hostile on future occasions. But if this is so we see that the primary goal is *still the reduction of anger*. Hence it is a mistake for an author like yourself to see your point of view as inconsistent with those who directly aim to reduce aggression to begin with. The ultimate aim is really the same in both cases.

Very truly yours,
Barry Bricklin, Ph.D.
Clinical Psychologist

A good example of why many people sincerely feel it would be best NOT to fight

Six-year-old Marvin:

"Mother doesn't want any more fights in the house.
When we fight she feels like running back home.
Or she goes to sleep.

"When Daddy and Mommy fight, it sounds like a
big battle and they wake us up and I feel like
stopping the fight. I go downstairs and I ask,
'Who started this fight?' and then they stop—

"I feel like calling the ambulance when they
fight because Daddy got cut on his hands with
a sharp knife.

"Mommy cries when they fight.

"I am sick and tired of all this being angry,
I want some peace and quiet."

A good example of how hate, and fear of hate, may masquerade as love

One of the most frequent and indeed puzzling challenges people pose against the notion of a universal aggressiveness in man concerns those attractive people we all know who *look like* they have achieved the culture-valued style of being sweet, affable, pleasant, and friendly; and one can hardly imagine they have an angry bone hidden away in them.

Worse yet, that is, the more challenging is the question, insofar as some of these people do indeed get mad at times; it then seems entirely unfair to think of their otherwise-niceness as contrived or phoney.

In the face of such genuinely nice people, it *is* hard to speak of reservoirs of a constantly rearing, recharging anger and, yes, hate, that must be vented for healthy living.

And yet, in clinical practice, time after time we are confirmed in the conviction that the

smiling sweet

may indeed be genuine

but out of fear of,

and at the expense of,

even greater caches,

stockpiles,

of bombs

which they are so busy trying to keep under control, it takes a huge toll out of their lives, let alone upsets their loved one(s) at whom they are so angry.

The niceness is indeed genuine, but it becomes phoney and ingenuous when the good stuff is used to cover "another" account.

Here is a vivid example of this kind of dynamic in a mother-child relationship where, at a late stage of a treatment process originally developed around a teenager with a long history of serious underachievement, the mother was able, quite remarkably, to describe a secret side of herself from way back when her teenager was an infant.

Never entirely unknown, or unconscious, yet a most closely guarded secret from the woman to her own self, let alone to her family.

Perhaps more tenaciously guarded from consciousness or openness than a more usual unconscious theme.

She reveals how she was constantly fearful of something happening to her infant. And behind this fear there lay enormous denied hate of the baby.

I was like the opposite of what I felt.

I didn't want him hurt, even by the human spirit, so when I felt ugliness in me, I was gentle to him.

I can remember often rushing to the baby fearing something happened—*my dreams making it happen*—like dreams of his running out in the street and being hit by an auto.

Sometime, I would get the feeling of sticking pins in my baby—in spite of the overwhelming love I was feeling. I never could seem to get the two working in a way that made me a whole personality.

Also:

I was afraid of driving. I used to get upset at seeing a dead animal. In fact, I would have my husband warn me beforehand when he saw a dead animal in the road so I could avert my eyes.

It is interesting also to note a very dramatic dream reported by the son of this mother; years later he saw his mother carving up a dog on a meat-serving board!

In this writer's opinion, it would be entirely wrong to say

blithely, 1st-year-psychology-student-like, that this woman was *really* hostile but covering it.

She was, is, as I knew her, a genuinely nice person, yet, indeed, *also* phoney, and terribly invasively angry, and her faults were exaggerated by her very denial of them.

NOTES AND REFERENCES

It is a painful eye- and feeling-stopping experience to find footnotes and reference notes punctuating a book.

Yet, it is a necessary simple test of scholarship that the sources of past ideas and discoveries be identified; in the arts, too, and even more critically in the scientific process sequence of men coming one after another, each successive researcher checking, testing, debunking, expanding, rechecking, and retesting the findings of earlier investigators.

So while we have skipped footnoting and reference numbers in order to cultivate a more flowing reading, we consider it essential that such reference sources be available to the reader.

In those cases where works were explicitly credited to the name of the author in our text, citations will be found simply enough in the alphabetical list of references.

However, there are also numerous instances where we referred to an idea that does have a significant background for us in another person's work, but without citing the name of the author. Also, all of the quotations we have cited need to have specific page numbers identified as well as the overall reference citation.

To direct the reader to these kinds of information, we append the following notes keyed largely to our "first book" of theory-building in which the information or quotation appeared.

We are not including such notes for virtually all the second, much more journalistic "book" of ideas for everyday living, but the professional reader should be able easily to identify in the references various links to the literature.

NOTES

Chapter one

page 33

1. Greenwald, H., "Marriage as a non-legal voluntary association," 1967, p. 8.
2. Satir, V., "Marriage as a statutory five year renewable contract," 1967, pp. 8–9.

page 34

3. Mead, M., *Life* magazine, August 23, 1968, p. 34.
4. The two most significant works on marriage in recent years, Bach and Wyden, *The Intimate Enemy: How to Fight Fair in Love and Marriage*, 1969, and Lederer and Jackson, *The Mirages of Marriage*, 1968, both offer a statistic of *one out of three* marriages in the U.S. ending in divorce!
An informed estimate is that if one removes from this figure all but first divorces—for there is a sizable group of people who go on to several divorces in their lifetime—the figure drops significantly, but still to some percentage point over 20%, or close to the "old figure" of 1 out of 4 marriages that we used to cite overall until recent years (Thomas P. Monahan. Address at American Association of Marriage & Family Counselors, Washington, D.C., March, 1971).

page 35

5. For a lovely, lively exposition of a proposition (sic!) for healthy extramarital affairs, this by an Establishment-type, former chairman of the Dept. of Psychiatry at Temple University School of Medicine, see English, O. S., "Conversation with a young married woman." *Voices: The Art and Science of Psychotherapy*, 1966; and for a lively debate concerning the proposition that affairs are or can be good for you, see the magazine debate of the same English and colleague, Heller (see references).
6. Ackerman, N. W., "The family approach to marital disorders." *The Psychotherapies of Marital Disharmony* (Ed. B. L. Greene), 1965, p. 154.

189

page 37

7. For presentation of the concept of pseudomutuality, see Wynne, L. C., et al., "Pseudomutuality in the family relations of schizophrenics." *Psychiatry*, 1958.

8. Dicks, H. V., *Marital Tensions*, 1968, p. 73.

page 38

9. Bernard, J., "The adjustments of married mates." *Handbook of Marriage and the Family* (Ed. H. T. Christensen), 1964, p. 732.

page 39

10. For shameless statistics of man's shame, see Richardson, L. F., *Statistics of Deadly Quarrels*, 1960.

Chapter two

page 42

1. Vaughn, J., 1967, pp. 4–5. (See references.)

page 44

2. Mudd, E., "Counseling couples in conflict marriages." *The Psychotherapies of Marital Disharmony*, 1965, p. 20.

3. For an example of a study which demonstrates the elemental significance of communication in marriage, see Naureen, L., "Communication and adjustment in marriage." *Family Process*, 1967.

4. Pollak, O., "Sociological and psychoanalytic concepts in family diagnosis." *The Psychotherapies of Marital Disharmony*, 1965.

page 45

5. Pollak, O., "The outlook for the American family." *Journal of Marriage and the Family*, 1967, p. 203.

page 46

6. Giovachini, P. L., "The treatment of marital disharmonies, the classical approach." *The Psychotherapies of Marital Disharmony*, 1965, p. 46.

page 47

7. Satir, *Conjoint Family Therapy: A Guide to Theory and Technique*, 1964, p. 9 and p. 11.

8. Ibid., p. 12.

page 48

9. Kubie, L., "Psychoanalysis and marriage: practical and theoretical issues." *Neurotic Interaction in Marriage* (Ed. V. W. Eisenstein), 1965, p. 10.

Chapter three

page 50

1. See Saul, L. J., *The Hostile Mind: The Sources and Consequences of Rage and Hate*, 1956, for a brilliantly down-to-earth psychoanalytic description of hostile distortions in child rearing, and at the same time a treatment of the larger problem of hostility in man. Should one need or want references to man's bizarre record of persecutions, see *Children's Drawings and Poems from Theresienstadt Concentration Camp, 1942–1944*; Darley, J. M., "Bystander intervention in emergencies: diffusion of responsibility." *Journal of Personality & Social Psychology*, and "When will people help in a crisis?" *Psychology Today*, 1968, on man as a bystander; Goya, F., *The Disasters of War*, 1967, for his series of sketches of war's disasters; Weiss, P., *The Investigation*, 1967, for a play of investigation of all of us; and Wharton, J. F., "En route to a massacre." *Saturday Review*, 1967, on how man is always "en route to a massacre"!

2. The midtown Manhattan study will be found in Srole, L., et al., *Mental Health in the Metropolis: The Midtown Manhattan Study*, 1962.

For a courageously open view of the marital lives of some psychotherapists, see the remarkable collection, "Staying married to a therapist: letters from wives" in the 1966 *Voices* issue devoted to marriage.

Chapter four

page 58

1. See Rheingold, J., *The Fear of Being a Woman: A*

Theory of Maternal Destructiveness, 1964, and Rheingold, J., *The Mother, Anxiety, and Death: The Catastrophic Death Complex*, 1967, and for a review of both, see Charny, *Psychotherapy: Theory, Research & Practice*, 1969b.

page 59

2. Bach and Wyden, 1969, pp. 350–351 and p. 355.

Chapter five

page 64

1. Grotjahn, M., *Psychoanalysis and the Family Neurosis*, 1960, p. 350.

2. Dreikurs, R., "Determinants of changing attitudes of marital partners toward each other." *The Marriage Relationship: Psychoanalytic Perspectives* (Eds. S. Rosenbaum and I. Alger), 1968, p. 99.

Chapter six

page 66

1. The correlation of love bonding with aggression in animals is based on the famous presentation of Lorenz, K., *On Aggression*, 1966.

Chapter seven

page 75

1. For an effective presentation of the deprivation, pain-inducing process of psychoanalysis, see Menninger, K., *Theory of Psychoanalytic Technique*, 1958.

2. For a beautiful description of the pain-inducing process of Zen, see Maupin, E. W., "Zen Buddhism: a psychological review." *Journal Consulting Psychology*, 1962.

page 76

3. A discussion of the confrontation process in family psychotherapy will be found in Charny, "Integrated individual and family psychotherapy." *Family Process*, 1966.

page 77

4. Rubenstein, R. L., *After Auschwitz: Radical Theology and Contemporary Judaism*, 1966, p. 128.

Chapter eight

page 80

1. Warkentin and Leland in *Voices*, 1965, p. 4.
2. Warkentin and Whitaker, "The secret agenda of the therapist doing couples therapy." *Family Therapy and Disturbed Families* (Eds. G. H. Zuk and I. Boszormenyi-Nagy), 1967, pp. 241–242.

page 81

3. Wheelis, A., in *Voices*, 1966, p. 46.

page 83

4. Winter, G., *Love and Conflict: New Patterns in Family Life*, 1961, p. 105 and p. 118.

Chapter nine

page 86

1. Cohen, R. L., "The adaptive efforts of the family to cultural change," 1969, p. 23.

page 87

2. Wiesel, E., "Jewish values in the post-holocaust future." *Judaism*, 1967, p. 268.

Chapter twenty

page 171

1. See Berg, I. A., "Cultural trends and the task of psychology." *American Psychologist*, 1965. And Feiffer's play, *Little Murders*, for a sardonic glimpse of how bad it can get for us everyday civilized people. Also, see Hannah Green's *I Never Promised You A Rose Garden* for a beautiful and deep picture of the inner man in all of us, and the awesome challenge of mastering our sense of our power—for good living.

REFERENCES

ACKERMAN, N. W. "The family approach to marital disorders." In B. L. GREENE (Ed.) *The Psychotherapies of Marital Disharmony.* New York: Free Press, 1965, pp. 153–168.

ARD, B. N., JR. & ARD, C. C. (Eds.) *Handbook of Marriage Counseling.* Palo Alto, California: Science & Behavior Books, 1969.

ARDREY, R. *The Territorial Imperative.* New York: Atheneum, 1966.

BACH, G. In Symposium, Hate and aggression. *Voices: The Art & Science of Psychotherapy,* 1965, *1.*

————. Thinging: a subtheory of intimate aggression derived from spouse-killings. In Symposium, Murder within the family. Presented to the American Psychological Association, Washington, D.C., 1967, mimeo. (See also Bach & Wyden.)

BACH, G. R., & WYDEN, P. *The Intimate Enemy: How to Fight Fair in Love and Marriage.* New York: Wm. Morrow, 1969.

BERG, I. A. "Cultural trends and the task of psychology." *American Psychologist,* 1965, *20,* 203–307.

BERNARD, J. "The adjustments of married mates." In H. T. CHRISTENSEN (Ed.) *Handbook of Marriage and the Family.* Chicago: Rand McNally, 1964, pp. 675–739.

BERNE, E. *Games People Play: The Psychology of Human Relationships.* New York: Grove, 1964.

BETTLEHEIM, B. "Violence: a neglected mode of behavior." In M. E. WOLFGANG (Ed.) *Patterns of Violence. The Annals of the American Academy of Political and Social Science,* 1966, *364,* 50–59.

BOWEN, M. "The use of family theory in clinical practice." In B. N. ARD, JR. & C. C. ARD (Eds.) *Handbook of Marriage Counseling,* ibid., pp. 139–168.

BRICKLIN, B., & BRICKLIN, P. *Strong Family—Strong Child.* New York: Delacorte, 1970.

BROWN, N. O. *Life against Death: The Psychoanalytical Meaning of History.* New York: Random House, 1959.

CHARNY, I. W. "Family interviews in redefining a 'sick' child's role in the family problem." *Psychological Reports,* 1962, *10,* 577–578.

———. "Regression and reorganization in the 'isolation treatment' of children: a clinical contribution to sensory deprivation research." *Journal Child Psychology & Psychiatry,* 1963, *4,* 47–60.

———. "Integrated individual and family psychotherapy." *Family Process,* 1966, *5,* 179–198.

———. "The psychotherapist as teacher of an ethic of nonviolence." *Voices: The Art and Science of Psychotherapy,* 1967, *3,* 57–66.

———. "Teaching the violence of the holocaust: a challenge to educating potential future oppressors and victims for nonviolence." *Jewish Education,* 1968, *38,* 15–24.

———. *Individual and Family Developmental Review.* Los Angeles: Western Psychological Services, 1969. Manual. Folders of history forms: I. Counseling Objectives; II. Family Developmental History; III. Personal Developmental History; IV. Child Developmental History.

———. "Marital love and hate." *Family Process,* 1969, *8,* 1–24.

———. Review of J. Rheingold, *The Fear of Being a Woman: A Theory of Maternal Destructiveness* (Grune & Stratton, 1964); and *The Mother, Anxiety, and Death: The Catastrophic Death Complex* (Little, Brown & Co., 1967). *Psychotherapy: Theory, Research & Practice,* 1969, *6,* 145–147.

———. "Normal man as genocider: we need a psychology of normal man as genocider, accomplice, or indifferent bystander to mass killing of man." *Voices: The Art and Science of Psychotherapy,* 1971, *7,* 68–79.

———. "Psichologia shel hashmadat am." *International Problems* (Israel), 1971, *10,* XXXXI–XXXXVII. (Hebrew; with English summary: A psychology of normal man as genocider, pages 9–10).

Children's Drawings & Poems from Theresienstadt Concentration Camp 1942–1944. I Never Saw a Butterfly . . . New York: McGraw-Hill (no year given—Library of Congress number 64–1557367570).

COHEN, R. L. "The adaptive efforts of the family to cultural change." In *Proceedings* of the Centennial Institute at the Jewish Family Service of Philadelphia, April 14, 1969, mimeo.

COSER, L. A. "Some social functions of violence." In M. E. WOLFGANG (Ed.) *Patterns of Violence*, op. cit., pp. 8–18.

DARLEY, J. M., & LATANE, B. "Bystander intervention in emergencies: diffusion of responsibility." *Journal of Personality and Social Psychology*, 1968, *8*, 377–383.

———. "When will people help in a crisis?" *Psychology Today*, December, 1968.

DICKS, H. V. *Marital Tensions*. New York: Basic Books, 1968.

DREIKURS, R. "Determinants of changing attitudes of marital partners toward each other." In Rosenbaum and Alger, see below, 83–104.

EISENSTEIN, V. W. (Ed.) *Neurotic Interaction in Marriage*. New York: Basic Books, 1965.

ELLIS, A. *Reason and Emotion in Psychotherapy*. New York: Lyle Stuart, 1962.

ELLIS, A., & HARPER, R. A. *A Guide to Rational Living*. Englewood Cliffs, New Jersey: Prentice-Hall, 1961.

———. *Creative Marriage*. New York: Lyle Stuart, 1961.

ENGLISH, O. S. "Conversation with a young married woman." *Voices: The Art and Science of Psychotherapy*, 1966, *2*, 65–67.

ENGLISH, O. S., & HELLER, M. S. "Debate: Is marital infidelity justified?" *Sexual Behavior*, 1971, *1* (#1), 26–35.

FEIFFER, J. *Feiffer's Marriage Manual*. New York: Random House, 1962.

———. *Little Murders* (a play). New York: Random House, 1967.

FLINT, A. A. "Crisis in marriage—reification or reality?" *American Journal Orthopsychiatry*, 1968, *38*, 560–564.

FOX, R. E. "The effect of psychotherapy on the spouse." *Family Process*, 1968, *7*, 7–16.

FRAMO, J. L. "Rationale and techniques of intensive family therapy." In I. BOSZORMENYI-NAGY & J. L. FRAMO (Eds.) *Intensive Family Therapy*. New York: Harper, 1965, pp. 143–212.

FROMM, E. *The Heart of Man: Its Genius for Good and Evil*. New York: Harper, 1964.

GIOVACHINI, P. L. "Treatment of marital disharmonies, the classical approach." In Greene, see below, pp. 39–82.

GOODMAN, P., & GOODMAN, H. *The Jewish Marriage Anthology*. Philadelphia: Jewish Publication Society, 1965.

GORDON, T. *Parent Effectiveness Training: The "No-Lose" Program for Raising Responsible Children.* New York: Peter Wyden, 1970.

GOYA, F. *The Disasters of War.* Intro. by Philip Hofer. New York: Dover, 1967 (*Los Desastres de la Guerra,* Madrid, 1863).

GREEN, H. *I Never Promised You A Rose Garden.* New York: Holt, Rinehart, & Winston, 1964.

GREENE, B. L. (Ed.) *The Psychotherapies of Marital Disharmony.* New York: Free Press, 1965.

GREENWALD, H., "Marriage as a non-legal voluntary association." Paper presented to the American Psychological Association, 1967, Washington, D.C., mimeo.

GROTJAHN, M. *Psychoanalysis and the Family Neurosis.* New York: Norton, 1960.

———. "Dynamics of growth and maturation in psychoanalysis." In Rosenbaum and Alger, see below, pp. 341–356.

GURIN, G., VEROFF, J., & FELD, S. *Americans View Their Mental Health.* New York: Basic Books, 1960.

HUNT, M. *The Affair: A Portrait of Extra-Marital Love in Contemporary America.* New York: World, 1969.

KOHL, R. "Pathologic reactions of marital partners to improvement of patients." *American Journal Psychiatry,* 1962, *118,* 1036–1041.

KUBIE, L. "Psychoanalysis and marriage: practical and theoretical issues." In V. W. EISENSTEIN, see above, pp. 10–43.

LAWRENCE, D. H. *Lady Chatterley's Lover.* New York: Pocket Books, 1959 (Cardinal edition of copy No. 402 of signed limited edition of 1000 copies privately printed by author in Italy in 1928).

LEDERER, W., & JACKSON, D. *The Mirages of Marriage.* New York: Norton, 1968.

LORENZ, K. *On Aggression.* New York: Harcourt, Brace, & World, 1966.

MAUPIN, E. W. "Zen Buddhism: a psychological review." *Journal Consulting Psychology,* 1962, *26,* 362–378.

MEAD, M. *Life* magazine. August 23, 1968.

MENNINGER, K. *Theory of Psychoanalytic Technique.* New York: Basic Books, 1958.

MUDD, E., & GOODWIN, H. "Counseling couples in conflict marriages." In Greene, see above, pp. 27–38.

NAUREEN, L. "Communication and adjustment in marriage." *Family Process*, 1967, 6, 173–184.

NEUBECK, GERHARD (Ed.) *Extramarital Relations.* Englewood Cliffs, New Jersey: Prentice-Hall, 1969.

POLLAK, O. "Sociological and psychoanalytic concepts in family diagnosis." In Greene, see above, pp. 15–26.

———. "The outlook for the American family." *Journal of Marriage and the Family*, 1967, 29, 193–205.

RICHARDSON, L. F. *Statistics of Deadly Quarrels.* London: Stevens, 1960.

ROSENBAUM, S., & ALGER, I. (Eds.) *The Marriage Relationship: Psychoanalytic Perspectives.* New York: Basic Books, 1968.

RUBENSTEIN, R. L. *After Auschwitz: Radical Theology and Contemporary Judaism.* Indianapolis: Bobbs-Merrill, 1966.

SATIR, V. *Conjoint Family Therapy: A Guide to Theory and Technique.* Palo Alto: Science & Behavior Books, 1964.

———. "Marriage as a statutory five year renewable contract." Paper presented to the American Psychological Association, Washington, D.C., 1967, mimeo.

SAUL, L. J. *The Hostile Mind: The Sources and Consequences of Rage and Hate.* New York: Random House, 1956.

SAUL, L. *Fidelity and Infidelity: And What Makes or Breaks a Marriage.* Philadelphia: J. B. Lippincott, 1967.

SROLE, L., LANGNER, S. T. M., OPLER, M. O., & RENNIE, T. A. C. *Mental Health in the Metropolis: The Midtown Manhattan Study.* New York: McGraw-Hill, 1962.

VAUGHN, J. Address at a banquet inaugurating the Center for the Study of the Causes of War and Conditions for Peace, Utah State University, 1967, pamphlet, pp. 4–5.

Voices: The Art and Science of Psychotherapy. Hate and Aggression. (Whole number), 1965, 1, #2.

Voices: The Art and Science of Psychotherapy. Marriage. (Whole number), 1966, 2, #3.

WARKENTIN, J., & WHITAKER, C. "The secret agenda of the therapist doing couples therapy." In G. H. ZUK & I. BOSZORMENYI-NAGY (Eds.) *Family Therapy and Disturbed Families.* Palo Alto: Science & Behavior Books, 1967, pp. 239–243.

WEISS, P. *The Investigation.* New York: Pocket Books, 1967.

WHARTON, J. F. "En route to a massacre." *Saturday Review*, November 4, 1967.

WHEELIS, A. *The Seeker.* New York: Signet, 1960.

———. "The illusionless man and the visionary maid." *Voices: The Art and Science of Psychotherapy*, 1966, *2*, 34–47.

WHITAKER, C. A., & MILLER, M. H. "A reevaluation of 'psychiatric help' when divorce impends." *American Journal Psychiatry*, 1969, *126*, 57–64.

WIENER, L. "A treatment of phobias: hydropsychotherapy." *Voices: The Art and Science of Psychotherapy*, 1967, *3*, 28–33.

WIESEL, E. "Jewish values in the post-holocaust future." *Judaism*, 1967, *16*, 281–299.

WINNICOTT, D. W. "Hate in the countertransference." *Voices: The Art and Science of Psychotherapy*, 1965, *1*, 102–110.

WINTER, G. *Love and Conflict: New Patterns in Family Life.* New York: Doubleday, 1961 (Dolphin Edition).

WYNNE, L. C., RYCKOFF, I. M., DAY, J., & HIRSCH, S. I. "Pseudomutuality in the family relations of schizophrenics." *Psychiatry*, 1958, *21*, 205–220.

WYSE, L. *Love Poems for the Very Married.* New York: World, 1967.

———. *Are You Sure You Love Me?* New York: World, 1969.

about the author

DR. ISRAEL W. CHARNY is a practicing clinical psychologist in Paoli, Pennsylvania, on Philadelphia's "Main Line," where he directs a private group practice, Guidance Consultants. He also serves as a consultant to a variety of mental health services such as the Jewish Family Service of Philadelphia. On the national and international scene, he is active in a variety of organizations especially as concern the interrelatedness of mental health and peace researches. Currently, Dr. Charny is chairman of the American Orthopsychiatric Association's Task Force to Assess the Impact of Current Institutions and Values on the Mental Health of the Individual ("Quality of Life"); he is a member of the same association's Study Group of Mental Health Aspects of Aggression, Violence, and War; and he is serving as a member of the Advisory Council of the Consortium on Peace Research, Education, and Development centered at The Institute of Behavioral Science at the University of Colorado.

Dr. Charny freely confesses that his central interest is *not* so much in marriage or the family—for all of his personal stake in both as well as his professional interest in new techniques of marriage and family psychotherapy. Mainly, he is concerned with understanding the sources of man's unbelievable violence, and how man might yet evolve to commit himself to a nonviolent way of life. He observes wryly that the marital relationship is an excellent laboratory for study of small-group aspects of man's violent feelings—and actions.